T0208813

CAMPAIGNS DON'T COUNT

CAMPAIGNS DON'T COUNT

How the Media Get American Politics All Wrong

MARTIN GOTTLIEB

CAMPAIGNS DON'T COUNT
HOW THE MEDIA GET AMERICAN POLITICS ALL WRONG

iUniverse books may be ordered through booksellers or by contacting:

iUniverse
1663 Liberty Drive
Bloomington, IN 47403
www.iuniverse.com
1-800-Authors (1-800-288-4677)

Because of the dynamic nature of the Internet, any web addresses or links contained in this book may have changed since publication and may no longer be valid. The views expressed in this work are solely those of the author and do not necessarily reflect the views of the publisher, and the publisher hereby disclaims any responsibility for them.

Any people depicted in stock imagery provided by Thinkstock are models, and such images are being used for illustrative purposes only. Certain stock imagery © Thinkstock.

ISBN: 978-1-5320-1859-6 (sc)
ISBN: 978-1-5320-1860-2 (e)

Print information available on the last page.

iUniverse rev. date: 03/10/2017

Contents

Preface to the 2017 Update

The first version of this book came out in 2006. Because the book ponders specific elections as they occur, the time had come for an update. Chapters have been added at the end of the book – Chapters 14, 15 and 16 – for the 2008, 2012 and 2016 presidential elections.

Nothing else has been changed from the original. A few references in the original are outdated, such as the statement that history since the Civil War has seen three presidential elections in which the popular vote was won by a different candidate than the Electoral College vote; there have now, of course, been four. And all references in the original chapters to the record of Allan Lichtman's system for predicting the outcomes of presidential elections refer to the record only through the 2004 election. But I wanted to present the decade-old work and the new work at the same time, for anybody interested in looking for differences. In truth, leaving the original chapters unchanged is a statement: Just as Lichtman's system has not had to be revised with the passage of time (unlike some other predictive systems), neither have the analyses provided here of various elections and of the system's application to them been changed.

The Author

Preface

This little book has been in the works for two decades. Throughout that period, I have talked about its subject at insufferable length and have taken more shots in newspaper print at conveying its essence than any writer should expect to get on anything.

My first boss during that period was Hap Cawood, who, in hiring me, took a chance on an unusual resume and rescued me from a life of various difficulties, including poverty. He then made a world traveler out of me and fostered my career. He belies the public image of an editorial writer, showing more interest in the opinions of others than his own, if you can believe that. He makes "laidback" an art form and, in the process, teaches a lot to all who know him well.

Now there is Ellen Belcher—partner/boss—who offers more tolerance, respect and support than I have any right to expect, and helps keep the whole thing fun after 22 years.

Both have my permanent gratitude.

Feedback from colleagues and readers over the years has provided me with a great opportunity to see what a book on the subject would have to do, how it would have to confront the natural questions and intelligent doubts that people have.

Some readers have said they've enjoyed the subject. Others have been mystified, at best. Both reactions have served to keep me going.

Thanks, also, to the Dayton Daily News, the incubator. History is not the only thing that newspapers are the first draft of. The people of the parent company, Cox Enterprises, also helped, by posting an early version of this book online for the 2000 election.

One of the most fruitful decisions I made was to ask friend Anna Hebner to take the last read before I turned the book in.

Introduction: Defining Insight

Although this book is aimed at anybody with a strong interest in American politics, the group I'm most interested in reaching is young journalists. This personal note is aimed mostly at them. Reading it is not necessary for an understanding of the book proper.

I was in graduate school during Watergate. I was in my mid-20s and had been a newspaper reporter in several settings and had been through the Army (though not Vietnam). I was back in school for a year, with a specific goal, and it wasn't a degree, which I didn't get. My bachelor's in journalism left me unconvinced that I really had a college education. Professionally, I wanted to be, oh, let's say, David Broder, and I thought that book learning was part of the path toward that goal. I wanted to learn what academe had to say about politics, to find out if there was anybody there who knew something I needed to know.

I was well read in only one field (unless you count the history of baseball, as written for adolescents): contemporary political commentary. In an attempt to develop a world view that I would have confidence in, I read habitually the (then) liberal likes of *The New Republic, The Nation, The Progressive,* and, even more so, the work of William Buckley, the leading conservative opinionizer of the day. I read his work in his magazine, *National Review,* and out of it. So much did I read Buckley that one professor told me my writing style reminded him of Buckley, by which he meant—one could tell—not in quality, but in style. I'm sure many young writers have become cheap imitations of Buckley at some stage, but I wonder how many other liberals.

My reading habits left me confused well past the age when confusion is cute. The problem was this: If William Buckley and John Kenneth Galbraith (the prominent liberal economist and writer and frequent debater of Buckley) were both brilliant, breathtakingly erudite, colossally well read, and unmistakably decent in their motivations, and if they disagreed in all the great debates of the day as to what course would make this nation and the world peaceful, free and prosperous, then one of them was brilliant, erudite, well read, decent and deluded. Moreover, because he was so adept at proselytizing on behalf of his delusions, he was dangerous.

Either that or Buckley and Galbraith were both half right, that is to say, mediocre in their life's work: the accumulation and dissemination of political and economic insight.

Well, if one cannot turn to brilliant, decent, thoughtful, knowledgeable and erudite people in pursuit of a confident understanding of what's going on, where can one turn?

One possible answer, of course, is that you can listen to the Buckleys and the Galbraiths and then bring your own values and concerns to bear and simply make a decision about what you think is right. If the dilemma you're facing is which political party to register with, then this may be your answer. But for somebody for whom politics was near the center of professional life, somebody who would spend his life exploring it and communicating about it, there had to be something more intellectually satisfying.

The basic issue: how does one make the leap from mere knowledge (possession of facts and such) to real insight?

In 1973, White House lawyer John Dean told the Senate Watergate Committee that earlier that year he had told President Richard Nixon that a "cancer" was growing on his presidency. The next day, Professor Milton Rakove, a specialist in urban affairs, said this to his graduate class at the University of Illinois in Chicago:

"He's got to resign."

At first I didn't know whom the professor was talking about. But he obligingly explained to the blank faces in front of him:

"Nixon. He's got to resign. That's how this ends: Nixon resigns."

I was dumbstruck. Presidents don't resign. And Nixon had just been re-elected the previous fall in a 49-state landslide. And, though Watergate was, indeed, giving him all manner of trouble, few observers had raised the question of resignation publicly. I knew this. I was obsessed with Watergate.

But Dr. Rakove didn't simply raise the question. And he didn't simply make a prediction. He was making an announcement.

I searched my understanding of things for anything that would lead me toward the conclusion that Nixon must ultimately resign. I found nothing.

For months after that, I searched the expressed thoughts of people in journalism, academe, politics and elsewhere for any thoughts of a resignation, and I found almost none. As for certitude that Nixon would resign, absolutely none.

When Nixon resigned, a year and a half after Rakove's announcement, I thought of Rakove.

Specifically, I thought that's the kind of understanding of politics I want. That's the kind I respect. Not the kind that explains events after the fact. Not the kind that analyzes things. Not the kind that tells you what "factors" are at play. (I was getting to the point where even *I* could do that.) I wanted the kind that predicts things. Flatly, boldly. Correctly.

Prediction is what cuts through the crap.

Journalists and most other political people—including academics—generally treat prediction in politics as a game, a sideshow. Occasionally journalists venture into boldness when contemplating the future, but most often with tongue in cheek. Later everybody has a good laugh about who was wrong about what. If you make a prediction—whether it's right or wrong—you get credit for being a good sport, and that seems to be the only characteristic that gets measured.

But physicists can make predictions within their realm. They can say flatly what will happen when two objects collide, or something. They *really* know their subject.

Of course, we can simply take the attitude that politics isn't physics—that nobody ever said politics is an exact science—and leave it at that. But we aren't required to leave it at that.

Before deciding whether to leave it at that, we should face this fact: when the alleged political experts treat prediction as a laughing matter, they serve their own interests. They free themselves of a form of oversight, of one way their listeners might judge whether the "experts" really understand things, or whether they just sound good.

The "experts" in politics are generally accorded the "expert" label as the result of some professional achievement. They've been award-winning reporters for some time. Or they've written important books or won advanced degrees from prestigious schools. They've been consultants to successful candidates. Or they've been successful candidates themselves. They are respected in their professions. And if you—the reader—are satisfied listening to the people the professionals listen to, fine. But what if the professionals are confused as a class?

Many people have attempted to study political phenomena somewhat the way physicists study physics. We have a name for these people: political scientists. They—or some of them—look for patterns in political phenomena precisely so that (among other reasons) political events might become more predictable. This book is not a brief for or against these people. My own experience with them almost 30 years ago did not leave me believing they are the hope for mankind. I thought they tended to get bogged down in unfascinating issues, and that they ended up making predictions that were too hedged or too small to be interesting. Or just too obvious.

As a matter of fact, a fair number of political scientists have turned their attention to the primary subject of this book: how does one predict the outcomes of elections, and what do successful predictions tell us about how the political system works? But most of these predictive schemes do not go very far and, for other reasons, are not all that exciting. (Some are considered in Chapter 3.)

But suppose somebody does come along who can make really useful predictions about a broad range of races, and can make them early in the year. Shouldn't that accomplishment be taken seriously?

In the hard sciences, the ability to say that if A happens, B will follow is the definition of understanding. Why shouldn't it be in politics? If such ability is rarer in politics—because the science is softer—that's all the more reason the ability should be honored. It is certainly no reason predictive success—or the pursuit of it—should be laughed at.

Milton Rakove arrived at his insight through some combination of intelligence, knowledge and instinct. Unfortunately, those characteristics are not easily transferable. But some ways of arriving at insight are.

In 1984 I became an editorial page writer for the *Dayton Daily News* in

Ohio. In that capacity, when I wasn't writing the unsigned editorials that are presented as the opinion of the newspaper on the controversies of the day, I was writing what I thought were David Broderish signed columns. They were about local, state and national politics. In the editorials, I was a moderately liberal Reagan basher. In the columns—my love—I was often an ideologically detached journalist (as in this book). Some people think detachment is a stretch. They are wrong. Piece of cake. Since when is abandoning principles difficult?

I found, in fact, that writing a political column was the easiest work I had ever done. Because I had been following political events way too closely for 20 years and had been aware of the biggest events for closer to 30, I had all manner of historical analogies to make to current events, all manner of precedents to cite for current behavior. Besides drawing analogies, I highlighted ironies. Ironies are the most common commodity in politics. You trip over them on the way to work. Then you get paid for pointing at them. Nobody knows why.

Sometimes I stated opinions about the prospective course of political events, but never the kind of opinions that could be disproved. I didn't opine that one candidate would prove stronger than another, just that one would have a lot of support, or would get a lot of people mad. I wrote the kind of stuff that looks like more than it is, or that, at least, the writer hopes looks like more than it is.

The cowardice was particularly shameful because, if I had dared to make a real prediction and been proven wrong about something, I would have paid no price. Pundits don't get fired or docked or even bawled out for being wrong, any more than they benefit from being right. It's not about that. It's about sounding like you know what you're talking about.

That is too easy to be considered respectable work.

A fundamental rule of punditry is that nothing ever happens that can't be easily explained away. The rule is especially true when the subject is election outcomes. In long campaigns, many things happen that seem likely to help one candidate. Many other things happen that seem likely to help the other. Picking what you want to use after the fact as the explanation for an outcome is trivially easy—always, no matter what point you're trying to make.

If Ronald Reagan demolishes Walter Mondale, despite your

pre-election insistence that the American people are really more in tune with Mondale, you have a whole menu of explanations to choose from: people don't really know what Reagan stands for; half the people didn't vote; Mondale didn't articulate a clear liberal alternative. Another piece of cake.

If, however, Mondale defeats Reagan, and you are writing from, say, a conservative perspective and have been insisting for years that the American people are on your wavelength, the explanation for the election outcome is just as obvious: the liberal media never gave Reagan a chance. (Reagan was able to defeat Jimmy Carter in 1980—you would pretty much have to admit—but in those days the media never took Reagan seriously. They learned their lesson.)

As for the non-ideological, non-partisan pundits, they, too, are always ready for anything.

Mondale defeated Ronald Reagan so badly in one debate that if it had lasted 10 more minutes, it would have been stopped, because nobody wants to see a president get hurt. Reagan told a story that made no point whatsoever, except that he was seriously confused. If Reagan had lost the election, many pundits would have been perfectly content to say he lost it in the debates. It would have been obvious. The pundits had been treating debates as momentous, turning-point events for years. This would have just shown that they were right.

Somehow, though, the fact that the debates turned out not to matter—that voters turned out not to care much whether an incumbent president can debate—didn't result in a great number of newspaper columns expressing confusion about the outcome.

Not many writers said, "Mondale's debate skills, compared to those of his elderly opponent, put on top of his refreshing honesty about the deficit, his daring and galvanizing choice of a woman for vice president and his shameless but clever willingness to give the traditional Democratic interest groups whatever they wanted, should have been enough to bring victory. I can't figure out what happened."

Yet I knew in my heart that if Mondale had won, all those factors would have been cited as the obvious explanations. I knew I would have been doing it.

Eventually, you have to start to wonder about this profession. I had the sense that I was playing a game with no rules, which hardly mattered, because there was also no score. You just do it. Then you come back and do it some more.

After a while, though, you start to think maybe there should be some rules.

CHAPTER

1

Campaigns Don't Count

A question for those who follow American politics:

You know how, during election campaigns, there are all those political experts on cable television every night discussing the question, "What do today's events portend for the outcome of the election?"

Well, the correct answer is almost always "Nothing."

But, of course, the answers the experts offer are not usually "Nothing." Indeed, the offerings are almost always some version of "Something." The answers are, to be sure, likely to be somewhat hedged, to allow for the possibility that events to be discussed on some subsequent night might supersede the events of this discussion.

That is to say, the experts promise to keep being wrong right up through the election.

If the answers the experts offered were always "Nothing," that would pose certain threats to the ratings of the shows in question; ultimately, there would be no point in putting the shows on night after night.

However, the reason the offered answers are "Something" is not mere commercialism. The experts on non-commercial PBS and C-SPAN make roughly the same kinds of analyses as the experts on the commercial stations. And, after all, the people offering these "Somethings" are sometimes—even on some of the commercial stations—the most respected figures in their professions of journalism, politics and political science. They are ethically reputable. They are not simply pretending to have certain views. They actually have these views.

The same views show up in newspaper and magazine analyses. The views are, in fact, everywhere.

But they are wrong. That is the fundamental phenomenon to be discussed here: the people who are in charge of explaining American politics to the American people don't understand American politics.

It's not just the journalists. The academics who advise the journalists on politics—to whom the journalists so often turn for quotes and interviews—help shape the prevailing journalistic views.

Indeed, the politicians themselves and their aides, their pollsters and their media advisers, have the same perspective. It's the entire political subculture we're talking about.

And the views of that subculture have been sold to the American people.

The prevailing view of politics—to be outlined below—prevails so thoroughly, so universally that it is not even seen as a view or a theory. It is seen as common sense, as obvious. If it is never challenged, that is partly because there seems to be nothing to challenge.

Just for the sake of argument, though, let's say that what prevails is only a theory. That theory has several tenets.

It starts with the premise that campaigns are what determine the outcomes of elections, at least in reasonably close elections.

If, in the spring, we—the experts think—don't know who will win a certain election in the fall, the explanation is, obviously, that the crucial events haven't happened yet. They will happen during the campaign.

The surface appeal of that logic is overwhelming. That the logic is not questioned is not surprising.

This book will question it.

The political analysts also believe—almost as a subset of their belief in the importance of campaigns—that American politics is substantially about the manipulation of public opinion through the manipulation of images. It's about who puts together an appealing image, a good television ad campaign and successful "media events." And it's about who succeeds in determining which issues and concerns the reporters and commentators focus on.

Some analysts hold that anybody who does not understand that media manipulation is the name of the political game is naive. Others try to find a euphemism for "manipulation," perhaps "communication" or "education."

The analysts also believe that television is monumentally important in election outcomes, because television is the medium through which political images are transmitted and received.

They believe—with slight variations in intensity—that money is near the center of American politics, because money buys television time. Lately, they have started worrying about who is most visible on the Internet, who is most popular with bloggers and with organizations with big e-mailing lists, and, therefore, most able to raise money through this new medium.

They believe—again, with slight variations among themselves—that issues and ideology are important in elections, in the sense that campaigns are often won by the candidates who, with much attention to media manipulation, get themselves situated on the popular side of the hottest issues of the day, the issues the public cares most about.

They also believe that events that happen during a campaign but are really outside of the campaign can have an effect on the outcome. Will the economy tick up or down in October? Might there be a last-minute scandal? A new foreign crisis? All these are possibilities to be fretted about.

In sum, the emphasis is always on what happens next—or is said next or put before the voters next.

Therefore, the most common answer offered by political experts during a campaign to questions about how the election will turn out is some version of "It all depends" upon how things go from here.

Intuition tells us that an answer so hedged could hardly be wrong. But, in fact, such an answer is almost always wrong.

This book argues that if, during a campaign or a pre-campaign period, a lot of voters seem to be undecided, or seem first to be going one way, then the other, what will determine how these people vote is not future events. Past events will rule, along with current circumstances. It bases that argument on the degree to which successful predictions can be made about election outcomes without assuming (or knowing) anything about future events. These predictions derive from systematic consideration of past elections.

The reason some people are undecided even in mid-October of an election year is not that the crucial events haven't happened yet; it is that these events haven't been focused upon yet. The focusing takes place at different times for different voters, but for many millions in some elections, only in the last 10 days or so of a campaign.

The focusing does not take the form of study, of course. No argument will be made here that the American people know more about public affairs than they are generally thought to know. Indeed, something close to the opposite point is made: that the campaign events that the political community obsesses over hardly register on the consciousness of the American people, or, more precisely, that if they register at all, they do so only temporarily. They wash out by Election Day.

When that happens, universally known, pre-existing facts determine votes.

Though the rationale of the voters is not based upon heavy-duty research and analysis, it is nevertheless rational and respectable. It takes the form of undecided voters coming to terms with the fact that an election is actually coming. At that stage, these voters do not start paying respectful attention to the baloney of campaigns. (What an amazing and insulting assumption it is that they would; more about that later.) Instead they think, in a presidential race, for example, OK, setting the campaign aside, how are things going for the country—roughly, in general—compared to reasonable expectations?

If these voters decide one way, the incumbent party wins; the other, the challenging party wins.

This understanding of American politics is almost provable with fairly simple scientific techniques, and is overwhelmingly powerful in its appeal once it is entertained through a couple of election cycles.

If adopted, it would revolutionize—a carefully chosen word—the way American democracy is understood, and might even greatly change the way it is covered and conducted.

After all, if American electoral politics is not fundamentally about the manipulation of imagery and about what happens next in campaigns, what is it about?

What can happen to American politics if the operators of the political system and the analysts and the journalists get over their obsession with media manipulation?

Is it possible that a form of politics might develop that is less petty, more satisfying to candidates and voters, less suspect of corruption by wealthy interests, and maybe even more conducive to smart and decent governmental policies?

CHAPTER

2

Polls the Culprit

Let's start here:

If campaigns don't determine the outcomes of elections, why do people think they do? That people, in the media and elsewhere, think they do is not difficult to demonstrate. Politicians spend months of their lives in a four-cities-a-day lifestyle that is founded on the premise that campaigns are crucial. The candidates frantically raise as much money for campaigns as they can. They choose their media consultants and their ads the way serious runners choose their shoes. Good, knowledgeable people devote their lives to the running of political campaigns.

The public buys in, if not by hanging on every word, then by talking (and apparently thinking) the same way as the pundits, when the subject turns to politics. Chit-chat around the coffeepot is as likely to be about how a candidate helped or hurt himself with a particular gesture or gaffe as about whether he's worthy to be president. C-SPAN, God's long overdue gift to the civically engaged, earnestly presents uncounted hours of coverage not simply of campaigns (an idea which cannot be faulted), but of professional campaign consultants lecturing eager college students on how to win campaigns. That campaigns count—and count greatly—is a given, an all-but-unchallenged, universal assumption.

And yet one can easily imagine a situation in which substantial skepticism about that assumption would prevail. After all, if campaigns count, then the explanation is that people's views are affected by what the politicians are saying—or are paying to have said in their commercials—about their own accomplishments, their future actions and their opponents' failings. But the American people are known to be deeply skeptical about what politicians say.

Indeed, general distrust of politicians is—and is widely seen as—one of the central characteristics of our political times. If it doesn't actually account for low voter turnout, it at least gives non-voters a socially acceptable defense, such as the now tired, old line, "I don't vote; it just encourages them." Distrust of politicians explains the high-frequency mockery of politicians by comedians eager to curry favor with the general public. The politicians are always there, always a tempting target, especially because they—almost unique in the culture—have absolutely no defenders.

When President Bill Clinton was found to have looked into the camera and lied, and to have lied to his family and friends, and to have gone to court and—at the very least—misled and dissembled, his political opponents went after him and got nowhere with the public. Even when only 31 percent of the people were finding Clinton "honest and trustworthy," in an August 1998 poll by CNN, *USA Today* and Gallup, he was more popular than Congress as an institution. After the Republicans had dramatized, elucidated upon and obsessively reiterated the fact that the president couldn't be trusted, they had still left one central question in people's minds: what distinguishes him from other politicians?

As if the people aren't instinctively skeptical enough, reporters and commentators are always there to put them on guard, to point out that the game being played in a campaign is manipulation of the media and, thereby, the voters. Journalists like to point out how the candidate's remarks of today conflict with what he has done in the past, or how he didn't really answer the question today, or how he didn't even take any questions.

It's true that public skepticism of politicians as a class does not necessarily extend to politicians as individuals. In their home districts, individual members of Congress seem to be respected. And presidents in general are certainly respected. However, we are talking about how people respond to candidates during campaigns, that is, to politicians in their most dubious form. During such a period, public distrust of politicians is presumably at its greatest.

Let's take an example of a campaign event that was generally thought at the time to be important. Conventional wisdom held that George H.

W. Bush benefited in his 1988 presidential campaign from saying, "Read My Lips: NO NEW TAXES."

But an ABC poll in the month he took office (when people are particularly likely to put partisanship aside) showed 77 percent of the people simply didn't believe him; they thought he would renege. They liked him well enough. They just didn't take him seriously.

As we shall see, the voters elected Bush for reasons that had nothing to do with taxes—conventional wisdom notwithstanding.

A question stumped the political community after Bush broke his promise in 1990 and raised taxes: why didn't his popularity go down? After all, we had quite a parlay here. He broke a promise *and* he raised taxes.

One elegant explanation worth pausing over is that, while the media pay a great deal of attention to what candidates say in campaigns (at least to the juiciest things), the public simply doesn't.

Is it possible that when people said they didn't believe Bush about taxes they were not being honest themselves? Is it possible they were influenced by the promise but were somehow embarrassed by that fact and wouldn't admit it? Of course. Not trusting politicians is the socially acceptable posture. To announce that one *does* trust politicians would be to invite incredulity, if not derision. As will be argued elsewhere in this book, one of the treacherous things about polls is that people may offer an answer that is designed to make life easy for themselves, in part because they fear a follow-up question. In the current example, a person might worry about having to explain why he or she believes what a politician says. It is so much easier to explain why one doesn't: "He's trying to get elected." Nobody, after all, could argue with that. On the other hand, to say "I don't know. He seems trustworthy" sounds stupid.

However you interpret the poll about whether people believed the no-new-taxes pledge, you end up at the same place. Either people were telling the truth, and they don't trust the politicians, or they were lying because trust of politicians puts one in too small a minority.

At any rate, there is overwhelming evidence for the argument that we ought to at least *question* whether the public has enough faith in politicians to pay attention to their campaign promises, claims and charges.

But we don't seem to have any doubts. The importance of campaigns is a given.

One likely response from the campaigns-count fraternity is this: maybe most people aren't influenced by campaigns, but a minority is, a minority that's big enough to swing some elections.

By this analysis, our election outcomes are determined by our most credulous citizens. Given the intellectual emptiness of what most people see in most campaigns most of the time, those who are most easily swayed by campaign propaganda must be easy marks, indeed. But, as this book will argue, credulity and confusion are not the characteristics that stand out about the swing voters who determine the outcomes of our elections, not once you look at the pattern of the choices they make.

Anyway, the question of this chapter is not why doesn't everybody accept the notion that campaigns don't count; this is only the second chapter, after all. The question is why does everybody in and around politics *assume* the centrality of campaigns? Why is there no debate?

The answer is clear: the polls.

The Bouncing Ball Mesmerizes

The poll numbers "move" during the campaign. Sometimes they move enormously. That fact simply precludes any discussion of whether campaigns matter.

If campaigns always ended up the way they look in the first polls, (A) nobody would be surprised and (B) the universally accepted explanation would be that voters pay no attention to politicians during campaigns. It would seem obvious.

But big movement in the poll numbers is common.

Let us look at fairly recent presidential elections primarily, because those are the examples that most people are the most familiar with. If my facts are wrong or my arguments leave out crucial data, many people will know.

Sometimes the movement in polls happens very quickly. After the Republican National Convention in 1976, polls showed Gerald Ford trailing Jimmy Carter by as much as 25 points. Yet Ford ultimately lost only 51-49 in popular-vote percentages.

In 1984, though this fact became quickly forgotten, Walter

Mondale—who was eventually to lose by a landslide—actually pulled within two points of Ronald Reagan in Gallup and Harris polls taken at the end of the Democrats' convention. At the convention, Mondale had done two remarkable things. He had picked a woman for vice president and had promised to raise taxes. The people who argue—or, more frequently, assume—that Mondale's promise of a tax increase was politically harmful to him need to at least pause over this data: the only time Mondale made great progress in the polls was immediately after he proposed the increase, which got huge attention, because it was in his acceptance speech.

(The explanation for Mondale's rise was not simply that conventions always provide a boost; some don't. The Republicans in 1976 and 1992 and the Democrats in 2004 saw no boost.)

Let's look, also, at the course of the polls in 1992.

Bill Clinton was doing badly for most of the year, relative not only to George Bush but to Ross Perot. A *Washington Post* and ABC poll in late April showed Bush at 36 percent, Clinton at 31 and Perot at 30. It was, remember, the pathetic condition of the Democrats—confronted with an apparently vulnerable president—that, according to Perot, fostered Perot's entry into the race in the first place. All the big-name Democrats had decided not to seek the presidency. Clinton was winning the nomination by semi-default over a weak field, despite being damaged by his dodging of the draft, his commitment of adultery, his discredited public denial of that, and the charge of corruption on an investment referred to as Whitewater. Qualms about his character were widespread.

But the Democratic convention—which came before that of the GOP—resulted in a huge gain for Clinton, in fact a big lead, which he never lost. A CNN/*USA Today*/Gallup Poll had Clinton behind Bush by 8 points a couple of weeks before the Democratic convention and ahead by 18 after. When Perot (temporarily) withdrew from the race in the summer, he cited the resurgence of the Democrats as one reason.

So the fluctuations happen often.

It is perfectly reasonable and natural to ponder why. And once one does that pondering, the importance of campaign events begins to loom large. After all, what else could be moving the numbers?

Really, though, it just doesn't much matter what moves the numbers. Tracking changes in the public "mood" is often not a worthwhile undertaking. The word "mood" is in quotation marks here not only because it is often used by the people reporting these polls, but because it may be an inaccurate word for what is being measured. In early 1991, the American military drove Iraq's Saddam Hussein out of Kuwait, thus driving George Bush's approval rating in the polls toward 90 percent. In 1992, however, Bush got only 39 percent of the popular vote, though his opponents were damaged and dubious.

Are the American people really so "moody" as to think in the spring of 1991 that Bush's presidency was a success and by the late summer of 1992 that just about anybody any party might nominate would do better? After all, not much happened concretely between mid-1991 and late 1992, other than the passage of time after the military victory, and the fact that the American economy improved, which would normally be expected to move the numbers in favor of the president. (In mid-1991, the country was in a recession. In late 1992, it was not.)

If these changes in the polls reflected changes in the public's mood, then the country had a bigger problem than the deficit, crime, drugs, poverty and family-breakup combined. It had an electorate that didn't know what it valued, that wanted one thing one day and something else the next. It had an electorate that, if it were an individual, would be a candidate for mood-controlling drugs.

In truth, however, many polls measure not moods, but vague inclinations, hunches and reflexive responses to immediate stimuli (in the form of questions). The pollsters are getting top-of-the-head, shrug-of-the-shoulder responses to questions the respondents may not have given a moment's thought before.

So, of course, the most recent events in the news affect the polls.

Ask somebody in the wake of the Gulf War what he thinks of George Bush, and, unless the respondent is a very unusual person, what comes to mind is the Gulf War and the commander in chief's apparently wise handling of it. Indeed, the respondent probably interprets the question as being about the war, because he is unable to think of anything else the (relatively inactive) president had done. So he gives the guy a thumbs up.

Now, of course, the political community understood when Bush's poll numbers went sky high in 1991 that they had to come down. But nobody—really, darn near nobody—realized how far and how fast they would come down, and how little would be necessary to bring them down. It became conventional wisdom in 1991 that Bush would be hard to beat in 1992. (Conventional wisdom, thy name is polls.) That fact is universally cited as the reason the big names in the Democratic Party (Mario Cuomo, Bill Bradley, Sam Nunn) decided not to seek the presidency.

The reason the political people didn't understand Bush's vulnerability was that they saw a mood—not a shrug of the shoulders—at work in the polls, and they couldn't see what would happen to change the mood suddenly.

They thought that something that might reasonably be called "public opinion" existed in 1991 about the election of 1992; it didn't.

The so-called experts are always quick to say that election polls provide only a "snapshot" of the electorate's views. But even that metaphor grossly overstates the usefulness of early campaign polls. What we are likely to get, really, is a blurry, awful, underdeveloped snapshot, one in which we can't even tell what we're looking at.

Questions Create Opinions

The astute reader will have noticed that I, nevertheless, use polls to make some points. Well, there are polls and there are polls. The argument here is not that polls are inherently bad, only that they must be understood and used carefully.

Actually, most of the common criticisms of polls are bunk. Generally, pollsters are intellectually honest. They are not artfully designing questions to get certain responses. And they are not picking respondents artfully, with political motivations, but are really trying to get a representative cross section of the people. Moreover, if they succeed in doing that—and they do know how—the responses they get really do give an excellent feel for what they would get if they were able to ask everybody in the population the same questions. That's hard for some people to believe when the number of respondents to a poll is only 1,500, or smaller; but it's true.

But if you know how the public in general would answer the question, you still don't necessarily know much.

The pollster asks somebody (or, if it were possible, everybody) a question. A response ensues. We call that response an opinion. But if the view expressed in the response didn't exist until the question was asked—and if the person never would have expressed it without being asked, and would never act on it—should we even use the word "opinion"?

The pollsters give respondents a "no opinion" or "don't know" option, and they would like us to believe that this takes care of the fact that some people have "no opinion." But think about the polling process: A questioner is going down a list of questions. If you are the respondent, do you want to keep answering "don't know," "no opinion," or "5" on a scale of 10? It seems almost rude, and it makes you look stupid. At any rate, you feel as though you are being asked by the person on the phone to think about the questions. It seems a reasonable enough request, and you have, after all, agreed to participate. So you think about the questions, and you obligingly offer the fruits of your instantaneous labor.

You may not think you're doing anything worth doing. The pollsters and journalists think you are.

If, in a particular campaign—or in the pre-campaign period—the polls are fluctuating violently, what that should tell us mainly is not that this or that kind of event has an effect on public opinion, but that nothing that should be called public opinion really exists yet.

When people have real opinions, they certainly don't change them because of the kind of dubious input they get from campaigns.

Why, in 1992, did Bill Clinton get a great "bounce" in the polls out of the Democratic National Convention, while George Bush failed to get one out of the Republican convention? (A *Washington Post* and ABC poll concluded that Bush got a 6-point "bump," but other polls showed even that evaporating in a few days, which is not the norm with these things.)

The political media addressed this question head-on at the time and generally concluded that many Americans had found the Republican convention off-putting. Nativist, isolationist Pat Buchanan—Bush's opponent in the primaries—had given a prime-time speech about the necessity to "take back" the country from forces corrupting its culture. Other speakers had concentrated on assaulting the Democrats, especially on "family values." It all seemed so negative, or so this theory goes. "GOP Sees Its Stress on Values Backfire" was the headline on a *Boston Globe* analysis on August 27.

The Democratic convention, on the other hand, evoked the future and embraced everybody, giving off warm vibes. So the theory goes.

It's important to pause over the state of the polls after the conventions, because the lead never changed hands again. Actually, never since 1948 has the lead in a presidential campaign clearly and convincingly changed hands after the conventions, though it has sometimes shrunk sharply. Conventions seem to be crucial. So whatever caused the Democrats to benefit and the Republicans not to benefit is also apparently crucial.

To accept the theory that the Republicans simply had a bad convention in 1992 is to accept the image-manipulation-is-everything theory of politics. Let us consider another theory. It cannot be proven here. But it ought to be borne in mind, at least, because it has a strong logic, and because it suggests that a very different dynamic is at work.

The theory: public opinion about Bill Clinton was not well formed before the Democratic convention, and therefore was still fluid, but opinions about George Bush were well in place by the time the Republicans met.

Before the conventions, Clinton had not spent much time on the national stage, and when he was there he was mainly dealing with embarrassments relating to sex and the draft. At the convention, however, the American people saw other sides of him. They saw a major national party embrace him enthusiastically. They saw his accomplishments highlighted, and they saw him behave presidentially. In short, they saw— if not a guy they just had to have—at least a respectable alternative to the Republicans. And they were more than open to the idea of change, because the country was not thriving under Bush.

Bush had been president for four years, so could hardly get much better known. The economy had been sour through almost all of his term; when it was not in recession, it was growing only weakly. The deficit was out of control. The crack-cocaine epidemic had fostered crime. Almost all the measures of a society's success were going the wrong way (except in the area of foreign policy). And the government wasn't doing much about it. Before George Bush became president, the term "gridlock" referred to road traffic; on his watch, it became a political term. Voters were so upset they were willing to consider Ross Perot for president. This was the sour period of American political history that saw the term-limits movement flourish.

There comes a time for any candidate when more talk can't do much.

That was what happened to Bush. The public had made up its mind about him before the conventions. It had just not decided whether Clinton was a respectable alternative.

Admittedly, this theory is phrased above in a way that seems to put importance on media manipulation: The public "saw" a different Clinton at the convention. He was the same man as before the convention, after all.

Obviously, what the public sees is not completely irrelevant. But all the Democratic convention did was the inevitable: It completed the picture of Clinton. It showed that he was not *only* a draft-dodging adulterer. It showed that he had had a serious career and that a lot of serious people who knew him well thought very highly of him. The convention didn't successfully sell the public a bill of goods about an alleged superman; it just made clear that the choice between Clinton and Bush was between two capable and flawed men. In that context in 1992, the choice would go to the new guy. The baloney of political propaganda had no impact; the real meat of the situation did.

If the Republicans didn't get a bounce out of their convention, it was because there was no way. How in the world could they have delivered a glowing, optimistic, heart-warming message about what a second Bush term would mean for the country, given the nature of the first term? To think that the convention planners could have pulled that off is to assign way too much ability and influence to the media manipulators, and to be way too cynical about the gullibility of the American people. It is to embrace the obsession with media manipulation that is the cornerstone of conventional political wisdom in our time. It is to ignore the importance of the important facts.

In 2004, John Kerry failed to get a bump out of his convention, failed to break the longstanding virtual tie in the polls with President George W. Bush. Why? The party was united, after all. And his speech was well-reviewed at the time, with Kerry showing a liveliness not always associated with him. And the convention made sure to avoid polarizing messages like Buchanan's.

When the poll numbers came in, Kerry's critics said the convention had been too focused on his military career, and his speech had been too lacking in a concrete message, had failed to communicate a galvanizing policy direction.

More likely, in the circumstances that prevailed in 2004, he had simply reached his potential in public acceptance before the convention. Hit the ceiling. There had been bad news coming out of Iraq, hurting the president in the polls, but there hadn't yet been much bad news about or for Kerry. Opposite of Clinton, he peaked early.

Let's look at the matter of "undecideds" in polls. Because of the polls, conventional political analysts do understand that some people make up their minds late. But what the conventional view of American politics draws from the presence of the undecideds is the notion that the last few weeks of a campaign are particularly crucial. Again, it seems a reasonable conclusion on the surface: if the voters are going to be making up their minds then, what happens then in the campaign must be decisive.

But we are not required by law to make that assumption. This chapter offers no contrary assumption, but a possibility, another theory:

Maybe what the undecided voters do at this stage is turn inward.

Few would argue that committed Democrats and Republicans are swayed by the events of a campaign. These voters know what they believe in, and they vote accordingly, campaign or no campaign, in accordance with their own values.

Why do we assume that the people who decide later are different on that particular score? Maybe they are just people who address the issue later.

Maybe there comes a time when the campaign gaffes of each candidate wash out the gaffes of the other. Maybe, by the end, so much information has come forth about both the candidates that open-minded voters cannot escape the conclusions that both are capable and both are flawed, and both are decent and neither is a saint.

Maybe all the occasions on which the late-deciding voters have heard one candidate make some sense have been balanced out by all the times they have heard the second candidate make some sense. Maybe all the impressive endorsements that one side has received have been washed out by the impressive endorsements of the other.

Maybe, at a certain stage, the voter simply starts over, taking a deep breath and saying, "OK, screw all that. What's the big picture?"

And maybe the non-partisan voters who determine the outcomes of our elections have a coherent and definable way of measuring the big picture.

Maybe, in other words, the small-picture forces that move the poll numbers are not the forces that determine the outcomes of elections. Maybe all the poll movement is irrelevant because it comes before the real heart of the decision-making process.

And if poll movement is what makes sophisticated people think that campaigns count, we are talking about a crucially important truth about modern American politics.

And it's a truth that the media generally don't provide to their audiences and that the political community itself doesn't seem to understand.

CHAPTER

3

Predict-Ability Found

I came across Allan Lichtman's name for the first time a couple of months after the election of 1986. It was in a small article in the *Washingtonian*, a magazine about life in Washington. The piece said that the man who had predicted a Democratic takeover of the Senate—with several seats to spare—in the magazine before the election had turned out to be right on 31 of the 35 races. Specifically, he called 53 Ds, saying he expected to be right within one or two. The Democrats picked up eight seats, getting 55 (soon reduced to 54 by a death).

That election was my first midterm election as a pundit. During the campaign, I had followed what the pundits were saying with excessive interest. Upon reading about Lichtman's success, I remembered my own amazement at the Democratic victory on election night.

Being focused already on the pundits' "predict-ability"—or lack thereof—I knew that none of them had been predicting what happened, not publicly at least. Indeed, the only good prediction that I had heard had come from the head of the Democratic national Senate campaign, Sen. George Mitchell of Maine. He was saying the Democrats might go as high as 53. The Republicans, too, were predicting gains—for themselves. In fact, the only person using the number 55 was Mitchell's GOP counterpart, Sen. John Heinz of Pennsylvania, who, at least early in October, was seeing 55 Republicans. All this according to the Oct. 3 *Washington Post* story, "Guaranteed: Heinz or Mitchell to Have a Red Face, Nov. 5," by Maralee Schwartz.

Even junior pundits know never to listen to what the partisans are saying.

Predictably enough, the media predictors were generally splitting the difference between the predictions of the two parties. The pundits' idea of analysis was to shave a little optimism off the partisan predictions.

However, rather than take any chances, in the last days of the campaign they were allowing for the possibility of one party or the other making gains. They said it all depended on what happened before the elections in the various states and at the national level. Their posture was understandable. Polls were showing close races all over the country, with more Democratic leads than Republican ones. In that context, seeing a net Democratic gain of a couple of seats—and a near 50-50 split—was not so much predicting as reporting.

I remembered, upon reading the story about Lichtman, that the main national news event that had happened on the final weekend before the election was the release of an American hostage in Lebanon. If, indeed, in the last days of the campaign, the outcome of the election "all depended" upon events still to happen, then surely a hostage release during a Republican presidency should have, at the very least, warded off a late national Democratic surge.

I was impressed most especially by the fact that Lichtman's predictions had been very early and had been unhedged. The overarching prediction about the shape of the Senate came in the spring. In a few individual races, he had to wait until September, because of late primaries. In rare cases, he also needed to wait for reports to be released about campaign spending, because that's one among eight factors he considers.

And he had made predictions in all the specific races, without calling any a toss-up, the great cop-out of other predictors who deal with the races one by one. That was particularly intriguing to a journalist.

Lichtman, after all, was not claiming to be an expert on the political situations in all the states that had Senate elections. He didn't know most of the stuff the local commentators were chewing over in the media in their efforts to handicap the individual races; that is, he didn't know most of the stuff they were saying the outcomes "all depend" upon. And yet he was making predictions that they wouldn't make, or, if they did try, couldn't do as well.

If Lichtman's success was not a one-time event, but something that could be repeated, the implications seemed to me to be enormous for political journalists. His work seemed to obviate most of what we do.

We agonize over television ads (does going negative work?), over debate flubs, over money, over personalities, over campaign organization and disorganization, even occasionally over positions on the issues. We do all this because we think this is the stuff that will determine who wins and who loses.

If it isn't, what is?

———

By the time I heard about Lichtman, I had heard about other efforts by academics to predict elections. These efforts weren't terribly exciting. For one thing, they didn't go beyond presidential elections. For another, they involved complex statistical formulas, which pretty much left me out.

Most important, they didn't have any great record for accuracy. Even by the 1990s, the science of election prediction hadn't come very far. Several high-profile systems—including those of two of the best-known names in forecasting, Michael Lewis-Beck and Ray Fair—predicted a Bush victory in 1992.

These statistical systems usually involve some measure of the economy and some polls, sometimes taken over a long period. The polls are likely to be about whether people approve of the incumbent president or about how people plan to vote. Typically, these systems yield predictions two to four months before the election.

The statistical formulas keep getting tweaked after every election so as to take the latest trend into account and yield a better prediction next time. By the mid-1990s, the science had made some progress. *The Washington Post*'s Robert Kaiser generated some interest in these systems with a front-page story on May 26, 2000. He noted that a half dozen systems predicted the Clinton victory in 1996, in some cases coming within a couple of percentage points of his vote.

Kaiser's piece was based upon the book, *Before the Vote: Forecasting American National Elections*, by James E. Campbell and James C. Garland.

But Kaiser's bottom line was, "Most of these models have picked the winner correctly in years since 1952 when the winner got 53 percent or more of the vote." That's not much of a claim. It left out three elections (1960, 1968 and 1976), meaning a 75-percent accuracy rate. (And the systems have problems with 1948, too.)

Getting a 75-percent accuracy rate is pretty easy. Just go with the incumbent party and you'll be right 60 percent of the time. Ask whether that party has a sharply divided convention, and you're up to 90 percent. That is, if the incumbent party is sharply divided at convention time, it is almost destined to lose (think of 1968, 1976 and 1980), and if it isn't, it typically wins. The 90-percent rate holds not just since 1952, but since 1860. (More on this in Chapter 5.)

Also, one measure of the economy—whether it has turned down during the election year to near-recession levels—yields about an 80-percent success rate since 1860. That is, when the economy has turned down like that, the incumbent party is very likely to lose; when it hasn't, the party is very likely to win.

Some of the systems that the *Post*'s Kaiser wrote about may, in a certain sense, be a little better than the *Post* suggested. One, by author James Campbell, in its 2000 form, gets all but two pre-2000 races right back through 1948; it's wrong about 1968 and 1948. (But it only predicts two months before the elections, by which time even the pundits generally have a clue.) Another gets only two wrong (1992 and 1960) back through 1956.

It's important to keep in mind, however, that the above-noted accuracy rates apply mainly to "predictions" done in retrospect. That is, you devise the formula in 1997 and apply it to the circumstance of 1952 to see if it would have worked. That's interesting to some. Obviously, though, "predictions" become a good deal more interesting when they are applied before an event actually takes place. But none of these systems have long histories of doing that, having really come into their own only in the 1990s.

Sometimes the systems go particularly far astray. Thomas M. Holbrook, of the University of Wisconsin at Milwaukee, predicted in early 2000 that Al Gore would win 59.6 percent of the two-party vote that year. No non-incumbent had ever won that kind of landslide.

One problem facing the scientists is that systems based on polling data and economic data can only be applied to races in the modern era, because the stats didn't exist earlier. That leaves the scientists dealing with so few races that any patterns they discern are likely to be fragile.

One of the researchers told reporter Kaiser that a system based on about 35 cases would be a lot better. So, if somebody could develop one based upon patterns that have prevailed since, say, the Civil War, when the current two-party system was born, he might have something. That is worth keeping in mind as we proceed.

Having said all that, these statistical systems deserve more respect than they sometimes get in the media. In the online magazine *Slate*, Karl Eisenhower and Pete Nelson responded to the *Post* piece with a series of criticisms of the statistical methods. One criticism was that the formulas only get the easy, non-close races right. In fact, though, journalists don't necessarily even do that. As will be noted at length later in this book, for most of 1988, the press most emphatically did not see George Bush's (easy) victory coming.

At any rate, I was looking for something a lot more interesting, a lot more compelling than the political scientists are offering even now, not to mention what they were offering in the mid-1980s.

———

In any election year, only a third of the Senate seats are up. And many involve incumbents who go virtually unchallenged. So a gain of 8 in the remaining seats is a major sweep. When the Democrats gained 8 in 1986, it was the biggest gain either party had made in about 30 years.

Early in the year, if you applied the rules of conventional political analysis, nothing said the Democrats would have a huge year.

True, midterm elections tend to be bad for the party holding the presidency, especially in the second term of a presidency. And the conventional political analysts are familiar with this trend. But the trend is strongest in House elections, which actually didn't go very badly for the Republicans in 1986; they lost only 5 seats.

Everything about the nature of 1986 suggested that the Democratic gains should be below average. The overall national situation was simply great, by any relative standard. The economy of 1984—which had allowed Ronald Reagan to run on the "Morning in America" theme—was still pretty much in sway. International relations were better than they had ever been in the lives of 50-year-old people, with the Soviet Union moving toward Glasnost and Perestroika under Mikhail Gorbachev.

Ronald Reagan was being called the most popular president in the history of polling. (The Iran-contra scandal—which put an end to his great poll numbers—broke immediately after the election.)

So why would voters be turning against Reagan's side?

The previous three times the president's party had experienced really major midterm losses in one house or the other in a midterm election were different kinds of years. One was 1974, when Watergate was humiliating the Republican Party. The time before that was 1966, when there was massive rioting in the streets of black ghettos and there was an escalating, controversial war going badly. The Democratic Party had the presidency and big margins in both houses of Congress; it paid a major price at the polls. The one before that was 1958, known in political history as a recession year. Of the three, only 1958 entailed major changes in the Senate, as opposed to the House.

In 1986, the Republicans clearly thought that Reagan was their best asset. He took to the campaign trail hard, focusing specifically on Senate races, saying he needed Republicans in the Senate to win confirmation of his Supreme Court nominees and to pass his Strategic Defense Initiative (the nuclear umbrella over the United States, which critics referred to as Star Wars).

Lou Cannon, in his book "President Reagan: The Role of a Lifetime," said, "In an extraordinary midterm campaign effort, Reagan had traveled 24,000 miles and made 54 appearances in 22 states, raising $33 million for Republican candidates." Cannon notes, also, that the White House thought its best bet in Senate races was to get an American hostage freed in the Mideast, which, as noted above, it succeeded in doing on the weekend before the election.

Even before the hostage release, the media did not see GOP chances looking bad at all. Typical examples: *The Christian Science Monitor*'s John Dillon on Oct. 30, "TV blitz may keep GOP on top in Senate." (Everybody was talking about the huge financial advantage the Republicans had.)

Paul Taylor, in *The Washington Post,* Oct. 27, "Fight for Senate Control, Resisting Any Trend, Stays Unpredictable." Taylor stuck bravely to his non-committal guns on Nov. 1: "Odds Stay Even in Battle for Senate."

Finding specific predictions on specific races in that election is not easy. But a magazine called *Campaigns and Elections*, put out for political campaign professionals, identified 21 Senate races that were seriously contested. It used a complex statistical formula to make predictions in all, and it was wrong on seven. That's three or four fewer than it would have been wrong on if it had flipped a coin in all 21 races and the rules of chance had prevailed.

But at least the magazine made flat predictions. At least it didn't deploy the usual "depend"-ent analysis, saying "it all depends" upon what happens in the hostage situation, or on whether certain candidates can come up with enough money to counter the last-minute claims against them, or on how the public reacts to new charges, or on whether turnout is high.

Lichtman, besides making his predictions early, made them without looking at any polls. He made them without contemplating campaign events to come. And he made them without any "depends" as backups.

If you don't look at polls, and you don't look at campaigns, you are flouting virtually all the tools of conventional political analysis. You are breaking all the rules that young would-be political analysts have to adopt to even get started in their careers.

And, more important, Lichtman was right.

Most important, he was making his predictions with a system that's there for others to use. By that I mean not primarily that it's easily understandable by laymen, though it certainly is. I mean that Lichtman's ability to predict doesn't result from some special, personal insight he might have into the future. That, after all, would be of no use to the rest of us. The *system's* the thing.

I may too often say that "Lichtman predicted..." But I mean, always, that the system predicted.

At the risk of sounding like some infomercial about a get-rich-quick real-estate scheme, the point about the system is that you can use it.

Yes, you! You don't need a Ph. D. You don't need a master's degree. You don't need to take a course in statistics. You don't need to spend the summer and fall on campaign buses, listening to the same boring speeches again and again. You don't have to consult endless numbers of so-called experts. You, right in your own home, can learn to SEE THE FUTURE not only as well as the so-called experts, but better. Yes, better! It's all right here, in this little book. And it's all absolutely free. That's right, absolutely free. No salesman will call. You won't end up on any mailing lists. You don't have to attend any dinners to get a hard sell pitch. Send no money. It's all ABSOLUTELY FREE!!!

CHAPTER

4

What Doesn't Win Senate Seats

Though his system borrows from science, Lichtman is not a political scientist. He's a political historian, originally a specialist in late 19th- and early 20th-century American politics. The story of his prediction schemes starts, as he tells it, when he met a Soviet geologist (yes, a geologist). They got to talking about the efforts geologists make to predict earthquakes and about whether those methods could be used in politics. The Soviet said that what geologists do is try to identify the factors that are sometimes associated with earthquakes, and then try to find situations where most of those factors are present.

That got Lichtman to thinking. In thinking about American elections, he made lists of the political factors he could imagine that might most often be present when an incumbent loses.

Seeing elections as choices between incumbents and challengers—rather than between Republicans and Democrats or between the left and the right—makes sense if you start with earthquakes and the question, what upsets the status quo. After all, the defeat of an incumbent is something like the political equivalent of an earthquake. Not that incumbent defeats are all *that* rare. But, in an earthquake, the "incumbent"—prevailing—peace is disturbed.

Lichtman, in preparing for the 1986 midterm elections, for example, looked at 132 midterm Senate races from 1970 through 1982 and asked if the factors that he thought might be present when incumbents (or incumbent parties) lose actually were. (Going back much farther than 1970

24

would have raised difficulty in finding necessary information, especially with regard to campaign spending, which he suspected played a role.)

When you look at his method, what's most amazing, perhaps, is that nobody ever undertook this exercise before. This may be science, but it is not brain surgery.

Fortunately for those of us who want to be able to play, too, Lichtman kept it simple. For one thing, he avoided matters of degree. He dealt in questions that could be answered yes or no, true or false. Is the incumbent senator running? (If so, that's a presumed advantage for the incumbent party.) Is the economy growing at a pace above a certain level or not?

Turns out the American political system lends itself wonderfully to the development of a predictive scheme that is based on historical precedents and is easy to understand. This is because the system is national, stable and binary. That is, New York has the same system as Alabama; you can use the same questions in all states' Senate elections. (National.) And the year 2000 has the same system as the year 1970, so you can keep the keys in play. (Stable.) And if we know which party lost, we automatically know which won. (Binary.)

If you've followed politics very long with much interest, you have seen references to schemes that predict the outcomes of presidential elections by looking at the Dow Jones average, or the unemployment rate, or at "peace and prosperity," or even at such fanciful elements as the height of the candidates, the length of skirts in a given year, the league of the team that wins the World Series just before the election in question or the length of the candidates' last names. These schemes—serious and fanciful alike—turn out to be decidedly limited in their "predict-ability."

Ultimately, however, what Lichtman did was simply combine many such schemes.

Of a serious nature, of course. After all, there has to be a rationale for a certain pattern, some reason to believe it will continue. No matter how many times elections have been won by the Democrats in years when the National League won the World Series, you probably wouldn't want to make any assumptions about that trend continuing. It looks too much like coincidence.

Anyway, for the record, the pattern only held in eight of 12 years in one recent, randomly selected stretch. Six of 12 would be nothing; eight of 12 isn't much. Meanwhile, the hemlines down/Republicans up theory held in eight of 11. (And Bill Clinton put to rest the notion sometimes heard among politicos that southpaws can't win re-election.)

The point of using several different questions is simple enough. If incumbents usually win, and people with some other factor going for them usually win, and people with yet a third do, then somebody who has all three is all the more likely to win. This turns out not to be mere theory, but reality. Furthermore, loose talk about the overriding importance of any one factor frequently ignores the possibility that several other factors of equal predictive strength may be pointing in the other direction. Best, obviously, to take account of all the most important predictors.

In Senate elections, Lichtman eventually found eight advantages that, among the many he tested, were most commonly present on the side of the victor in Senate races. There's nothing magic about the number eight. He simply found that if he applied more factors to the 132 races, he couldn't retroactively "predict" their outcomes any better.

He found that if four of the eight factors are present on the side of the party that already has the Senate seat, that party can be expected to hold the seat. If not, the other party should be predicted to win. Again, there's nothing magical about the number four. It's just what the study of the 132 races showed.

The eight factors have little to do with what journalists and pundits analyze to death during the campaigns.

If what is being presented here involved standard deviations and Nth degrees and regression analysis, then journalists could— and most certainly would—say it's all too complex for us and the general public to deal with. Maybe this professor has something, they might say, but we are going to go with our instincts, with "common sense," and with, as a matter of fact, the advice of the vast majority of experts, including most professors, which tends to confirm what we're calling common sense.

I know from having written about this subject for almost 20 years for newspapers, and having gotten some feedback, that journalists and political practitioners alike are eager to cop this attitude. When I promote the Lichtman form of analysis, I don't get much in the way of rebuttals. But many people do not want to believe the implications of the Lichtman approach, because it puts the lie to the analyses they have been making all these years, and because it seems to them to take all the fun out of politics, to make everything seem predetermined (about which, more in due course). So they say it's too complicated and academic.

Baloney.

The eight questions Lichtman asks about every Senate race that takes place in a midterm election—based upon the eight factors he has found to be the best predictors when standing alone—are listed below with some commentary, mainly about why they are good predictors.

The commentary is mine, not Lichtman's, and is open for debate.

A longer book than this one might look in detail at the predictive power of questions that Lichtman found wanting as predictors or at questions he might have neglected to test. But the point here is not that the questions he uses now are the best predictors that anybody could possibly have come up with. The largest point is simply that his questions—painstakingly selected and remarkably successful in making predictions (though more on that later)—are enormously instructive for what they don't include.

Most of the questions will not be amazing to experienced observers of politics. But the absences are another matter. Before you start looking at the list, you might want to ask yourself what you think the best predictors are and/or what the typical pundit might list.

The questions are phrased so that a "true" answer always favors the incumbent party and a false always favors the challenging party. This makes the phrasing a bit awkward at times. But the phrasing pays off in the fact that you have only to count up the trues to see who "wins."

In still another way the system is binary and simple: four or more "trues" and the incumbent party wins; three or fewer, it loses. There are no toss-ups.

The system Lichtman uses in midterm elections is slightly different from that used in Senate elections that are held simultaneously with a presidential election. Lichtman has found that the two kinds of elections have slightly different dynamics. The two systems each have eight questions, and the first six are the same. We start with the midterms.

Key 1 (Incumbency): *The incumbent-party candidate is the sitting senator.*

The meaning of this factor (or key, to use Lichtman's terminology), is not entirely that incumbents tend to get re-elected (which nobody needs Lichtman to point out). The meaning is also that if the incumbent doesn't run, the other party tends to win the seat. This is a tendency that I, for one, upon discovering Lichtman, had never seen highlighted in any piece of journalism I had read in my middle-aged life.

Key 2 (National figure): *The incumbent party's candidate is a national figure.*

National figures tend to win. The term "national figure," like others in the Lichtman scheme, is a judgment call. But the guideline is that the threshold is a high one. Ted Kennedy. John Glenn. Jesse Helms. Hillary Clinton. Walter Mondale. It's a judgment that can be made by politically alert laymen.

Key 3 (Contest): *There is no serious contest for the nomination of the incumbent party.* (Specifically, if there's a primary, the winner gets at least two-thirds of the vote.)

Party unity helps. This confirms conventional wisdom. However, see key 8; it doesn't work the same way for the challenging party. Why does it work this way for the incumbent party? The reader will note that the concept of personal stature seems to run throughout the keys. (Even the first two keys can be seen as being about personal stature.) If the incumbent is seriously challenged within his own party, that's an indication he lacks the kind of stature that incumbents usually gain from Senate service. If the incumbent isn't running, and a tough primary happens, perhaps that highlights for the public that the new nominee doesn't have the stature of the old incumbent.

Key 4 (Landslide): *The incumbent party won the seat with 60 percent or more of the vote in the previous election.*

A landslide victory is not often followed by a defeat. If the landslide was won by an incumbent who is not seeking re-election, even that bodes well for the incumbent party, because the landslide may say something about the strength of the particular party in the particular state. Note, however, that this is the closest any midterm key comes to taking into account the strength of a party. There's no key about party-registration figures or the party label of other elected officials in the state or which party has been carrying the state in presidential elections. Lichtman tested keys like that and found they were not very good predictors. The keys deal enough—indirectly—with party size to make clear that a Democrat has a problem in, say, Utah, where, for example, the 60-percent threshold is relatively likely to have been broken in the previous election. But where the difference between the parties is any less dramatic, party strength is not likely to be a very good predictor.

Key 5 (Money): *The incumbent-party candidate outspends the challenger by 10 percent or more.*

Some people will read this key as a vindication of the conventional wisdom about the importance of money in politics: the side with the money wins. However, the meaning of this key may not be that money wins. Note that the gap Lichtman is talking about is only 10 percent. A gap of that size isn't a great advantage, even by the standards of conventional political analysis, which is inappropriately fixated on money. The import of the key may be simply that if the incumbent party can't easily and dramatically outraise the challenging party, something is wrong. In other words, it's not that the flow of money in a certain direction causes something to happen, but that the flow tells us something about what is happening. After all, money tends to go to incumbents, because they tend to be expected to win, and contributors want to have a senator they have helped. If the money isn't going there, it's probably because the incumbent is seen as exceptionally weak. Sometimes candidates who are seen as weak actually are.

Key 6 (Credentials): *The challenging-party candidate is not a major national figure or a past or present governor or member of Congress.*

Again, the issue appears to be personal stature. The incumbent party is better off if the candidate of the challenging party doesn't have it.

One might be tempted to gather, instead, that the issue in this key is name recognition. But the inclusion of "member of Congress" in the list of qualifications throws some doubt on that, because most members of Congress are largely anonymous beyond their own districts. At any rate, name recognition is a dubious concept, if it is meant to suggest—as it often is—that people will vote for the name on the ballot that they recognize. By the time a closely contested Senate race is over, both candidates have almost universal name recognition in the state.

Most likely what's at work here is the feeling on the part of the swing voters that if a person has been around for awhile— playing in the big leagues—without self-destructing, that's an indication he might be trusted not to do something ridiculous in office. Candidates who, on the other hand, materialize just before a campaign have a respectability hurdle to overcome.

One often hears the notion that what a party needs to do in a certain election is put up a "fresh face," somebody who is not seen as a politician. One heard this particularly often in the early 1990s, when there was an "anti-incumbent" thing in the air. However, judging from the history encapsulated in the Lichtman keys, public distrust of politicians extends to would-be politicians.

Another factor making credentials important: Often when the challenging party puts up a candidate who is not well credentialed, it's because none of the big names wants to make the race. That might be because the incumbent is seen as unbeatable. That might mean that he or she actually is unbeatable.

Finally, I should add that "credentials" is my shorthand way of summarizing what this key is about. One can argue that experience in certain offices is an important predictor of success for other reasons: It demonstrates that a candidate has won certain kinds of elections before. That suggests he might be strong in the pending campaign, or that he has useful experience or contacts.

Key 7 (The presidency): *The incumbent party is not the party of the president.*
All other things being equal, midterms tend to be bad for the party that holds the presidency. (The last two midterms, 1998 and 2002, are either exceptions or the beginning of a new era on that score.) Many reasons for the midterm phenomenon have been offered by analysts: That non-presidential parties are freer to be irresponsible with vote-getting charges and promises. That members of the non-presidential party can run as individuals, and can shape their campaigns to their specific political

needs, whereas members of the president's party are almost inevitably in some degree tied to him, no matter what they do. That presidents are the easiest people to blame for whatever is going wrong.

Perhaps some of the swing voters who determine the outcomes of our elections look at which party is holding the most power (i.e., the presidency) and decide to limit that party. We are talking, after all, about voters who, by definition, are not fans of the ideology of either party. It is natural for them to want to balance the parties off. (That instinct doesn't seem too terribly powerful in presidential elections, though, when the party that wins the presidency also tends to make minor gains in Congress.)

Key 8 (Challenger contest): *There is no serious contest for the challenging party's nomination.*

In other words, the non-incumbent party is more likely to win if it has a hard-fought primary. This is the key that flies most directly in face of conventional wisdom, which sees intraparty division as bad. This key, Lichtman notes, is the least effective of the eight keys as a predictor when standing alone. Why is it a predictor at all? Why is a party better off to have a race that divides its people into large camps and consumes its money? Probably for two reasons: (1) If there's serious competition for the nomination, that probably means that a lot of people see the nomination as worth winning, because the other party is in a weak position. (2) Again, we get back to stature. A candidate who wins a hard-fought, high-profile, statewide primary is seen as worthy, somebody ready for prime time. The victory becomes a credential. Meanwhile, the fact that the party is divided in the primary doesn't particularly hurt the party in the public's eye, because the idea of politicians fighting for an open seat seems perfectly normal. It's when an incumbent is challenged within his own party that a party looks bad. (This distinction between challenging-party division and incumbent-party division is, again, one I had never seen made before Lichtman made it.)

Here are the two different keys used in presidential years. They are self-explanatory:

Key 7 (The presidential keys): *The keys to the presidency predict a victory for the incumbent senator's party.*

Key 8 (Party strength): *The party of the incumbent senator holds a majority in the lower house of the state legislature.*

The Senate keys are applied to some specific races in Chapter 8. But let's look at a couple of hypothetical examples here. They are useful in exploring not only the strengths, but the weaknesses of the keys.

In early 2000, the Senate race everybody was talking about was one that never happened. It pitted New York City Mayor Rudolph Giuliani against Hillary Clinton. (Giuliani withdrew.)

It had become the nation's Senate race. For the political pundits, the questions were mainly about Hillary: Was she too liberal, too much an outsider? Did she start with too many negatives, too many people who wouldn't vote for her no matter what?

The Republicans were eager to put up Giuliani for reasons obvious to anybody familiar with conventional political analysis: here was a Republican who regularly won elections in overwhelmingly Democratic New York City. The party leaders did everything possible to get other GOP candidates to step aside.

In a Clinton-Giuliani matchup, key 1 (incumbency) would have generated the answer "false," meaning it works to the advantage of the non-incumbent party, in this case the Republicans. Incumbent Democratic Sen. Daniel Patrick Moynihan was retiring.

Key 2 (national figure) would have gone to the Democrats; Hillary was obviously a national figure, not simply because she was the president's wife, but because she was seen as a national political force, somebody whose name would come up for the national ticket if she were elected to the Senate.

Key 3 (contest) also would have gone to Hillary; the other Democrats who might have sought the nomination stepped aside for her.

Key 4 (landslide) would have gone to the Republicans. Moynihan had not won a landslide in 1994. He won about 56 percent against the relatively unknown Bernadette Castro. The Republicans as a party didn't seem to be making a real effort, because Moynihan was seen as entrenched. If the year hadn't turned out so overwhelmingly Republican across the nation, Moynihan might well have cracked the 60-percent threshold. In 1988, after all, he got 67 percent. Nevertheless, the mere fact that New York leans Democratic would not have been enough to get Clinton this key.

Key 5 (money) couldn't be resolved.

Key 6 (challenger credentials) would have been Hillary's. The keys all but specifically exclude mayors as strong candidates. And, indeed, mayors of New York have demonstrated the wisdom of that exclusion by repeatedly failing to move up. The key can be turned for the challenger if he's a national figure. While Giuliani started out the race being well-known in national political circles, he did not, before 9-11, have much standing with the national general public.

Let's set aside key 7 (about how the presidential keys break, in the system relating to presidential years).

Key 8 (party strength) would give Hillary the fourth key she needed to be predicted to win. The Democrats solidly controlled the New York House of Representatives.

When Giuliani had health and scandal problems that resulted in his withdrawal, the first thought of many people was that Hillary was dodging a bullet. But Giuliani was replaced as a candidate by U.S. Rep. Rick Lazio. This got the Republicans key six back from Hillary.

Against Lazio, Hillary needed either key 5 (money) or 7 (the presidential keys) to win. But the Republicans outspent her $55 million to $30 million. (Let's continue to set aside discussion of the presidential keys.)

The keys seem to suggest that Lazio was a stronger candidate than Giuliani. This defies conventional wisdom. It even defies common sense. The Senate keys are not always right. Being based on historical precedent, they are particularly subject to being subverted by an almost unprecedented situation. Giuliani won the nomination by acclamation, on the premise that he was the stronger candidate. Then he withdrew, under rare circumstances, and the Republicans made a rushed decision. Yes, they got a member of Congress, but one who had already been judged a relatively weak candidate.

At any rate, the major claim to be made for the keys is not they can tell you who would have a better chance against Clinton. It's that they make a prediction in Clinton-Giuliani and in Clinton-Lazio that is very likely to be right. (Let's continue to set aside discussion of the presidential keys.)

———

Meanwhile, let's look at another hypothetical example:

In Ohio, in 1998, the state was halfway expecting a matchup of its political titans. Democratic Sen. John Glenn was up for re-election, and the very popular Gov. George Voinovich was planning to challenge him. The betting was generally on Voinovich. Glenn was in his late 70s. Republicans were winning everything in sight in Ohio (though losing the state to Clinton twice). Glenn was somewhat tarnished by minor scandals; he had won solidly in 1992, against an ordinary candidate, but not by a landslide. In 1998, it just seemed like Voinovich's time.

The election took place while Glenn was circling the air in space, as the world's first septuagenarian astronaut. That presumably would have affected conventional political predictions, if Glenn had decided to run, which he didn't.

Exactly how that factor might have affected the outcome is hard to say. None of Lichtman's keys asks whether a candidate is actually on planet Earth on Election Day.

Either way, the keys would have favored Glenn—barely. Incumbent. National figure. Unchallenged within the party. That's three. The fourth would have been key 8, which, in a midterm, goes to the challenging party only if it has a tough primary. Voinovich was the consensus GOP candidate, and was not going to be challenged.

As noted above, key 8 is the weakest of the keys as a predictor standing alone. And its logic didn't apply in this case. The absence of a primary reflected only Voinovich's exceptional standing. It seems odd that the Lichtman system should penalize him for that. Keep in mind, though, that the keys do give Voinovich credit for being governor, by giving him key 6 (credentials). Being governor *and* winning a tough primary would have been better.

When Glenn retired, all doubt was removed. Voinovich ended up with almost all the keys: No incumbent for the incumbent party. No national figure for them. The Democrats didn't have much of a primary, so they did get that key. But the landslide key did not go to them. Meanwhile, the Republican money machine was destined to blow away the Democrats, and everybody knew it. Voinovich got the credentials key, as a governor. He got another key for being a Republican in a midterm election in which the Democrats held the White House. He lost the most dubious key for not having a primary. Six to two in keys.

The system saw things the same way as conventional political analysis, and the race turned out to be a blowout.

———————

Play around with the keys awhile, and some interesting implications arise. Here's one: If you're talking about a generic senator—that is, not a national figure and not a landslide winner last time—he or she is surprisingly vulnerable. If, for example, the incumbent is running for re-election against a member of Congress in a year when the other party seems likely to win the presidency, the race comes down to money, according to the keys. Not counting money, the incumbent has lost four keys. One more and out.

Typically, incumbents should have money working for them, because incumbents have plenty of time to raise money and are generally expected to win. But if, say, an incumbent is a Democrat in a state the Republicans think they should have, or if he's personally seen as not very strong, he's got a major problem.

———————

The bottom line:

No claim is made here that the keys Lichtman has come up with are the best possible predictors. It may depend upon where you start, what guesses you make about what's important. Moreover, a researcher who is not so bent on keeping it simple—who is willing to deal in complex statistics and matters of degree, rather than insisting on true-false questions—might be able to come up with an even better prediction scheme. Suffice it to say that, in years of looking, I have never come across a system that achieves the success rate that Lichtman achieved in 1986.

The competition between Lichtman and other academic schemes is not terribly important for our purposes. The fundamental point is that remarkably good predictions can be made with:

- no knowledge of anybody's campaign tactics;
- no direct knowledge of the candidates' stands on the issues;
- no knowledge about the personalities of the candidates;
- no knowledge of the state of the economy either nationally or locally (Lichtman specifically tested whether economic factors make good predictors in Senate elections and found they don't.);
- no knowledge of whom the candidates have hired to direct their media campaigns or their campaign staffs;
- no knowledge of what non-campaign events might take place during the campaign and affect public opinion;
- no direct knowledge of what any of the polls say in September or October or any other time;
- no measurement of a candidate's "negatives" going into a race;
- no knowledge, in short, of all the stuff the alleged experts in and around journalism fixate on endlessly, of all the stuff the "experts" seem to think is most important.

Allan Lichtman's 13 Keys to the Presidency

Six or more of these statements must be untrue to predict that the incumbent party will lose the popular vote.

Key 1 (Party mandate): *After the last midterm election, the incumbent party holds more seats in the U.S. House of Representatives than it did after the previous midterm election.*

Key 2 (Contest): *There is no serious contest for the incumbent-party nomination.*

Key 3 (Incumbency): *The incumbent-party candidate is the sitting president.*

Key 4 (Third party): *There is no significant third-party or independent campaign.*

Key 5 (Short-term economy): *The economy is not in recession during the election campaign.*

Key 6 (Long-term economy): *Real per-capita economic growth during the current presidential term equals or exceeds mean growth during the previous two terms.*

Key 7 (Policy change): *The incumbent administration effects major changes in national policy.*

Key 8 (Social unrest): *There is no sustained social unrest during the term.*

Key 9 (Scandal): *The incumbent administration is untainted by major scandal.*

Key 10 (Foreign/military failure): *The incumbent administration has suffered no major failure in foreign or military affairs.*

Key 11 (Foreign/military success): *The incumbent administration has achieved a major success in foreign or military affairs.*

Key 12 (Incumbent charisma): *The incumbent-party candidate is charismatic or a national hero.*

Key 13 (Challenger charisma): *The challenging-party candidate is not charismatic or a national hero.*

CHAPTER

5

What Doesn't Win the Presidency

We come now to my favorite year.

As 1988 approached, I was not convinced about this Lichtman stuff. Intrigued, to be sure, because of the remarkable and singular success of his predictions in 1986. I sought Lichtman out for an interview. I wrote about his system several times between 1986 and 1988. At first I wrote very positively, as I began the process of reevaluating my own embarrassingly conventional understanding of politics. But as the 1988 election approached, Lichtman seemed quite clearly to be going wrong.

It turned out that he had a system for predicting the outcomes of presidential elections, too. He had first deployed it in the 1984 election. Of course, I wasn't much impressed that he predicted the re-election of Ronald Reagan, because everybody had made that prediction. Reagan coasted to a 49-state win over Walter Mondale. A good deal more interesting, admittedly, was the timing of Lichtman's forecast. He had written in the April 1982 edition of *Washingtonian* magazine a piece called "How to bet in '84." He said that Reagan looked strong.

The piece was written during a bad time for Reagan. Upon the passage of Reagan's tax-cut plan in 1981, the country had plunged into the worst recession since the Great Depression of the 1930s. By '82, the Republican Party was divided over whether to go back and raise taxes, what with the deficit soaring. Most Democrats (a category into which Lichtman fits) were in an I-told-you-so mode about Reagan, convinced that his ideological delusions were producing catastrophe for the nation. The midterm congressional election would see the Democrats gain 26 House seats (and one in the Senate).

One of the central notions of conventional analysis of American politics is the old "peace and prosperity" theory. By this theory, an incumbent president who runs during peace and prosperity is thought to be all but unbeatable, but a bad economy is held to be big trouble.

Yet here was Lichtman making his hedged prediction of Reagan strength at the depths of an unusually bad recession.

Of course, peace and prosperity did turn out to prevail in 1984. That obviously mattered in the outcome. But another factor often cited for Reagan's landslide was Democratic nominee Walter Mondale's allegedly excessive liberalism, combined with his overt ties to Democratic interest groups. Indeed, the Democratic Party itself seemed to eventually accept this analysis. By 1988, the party was trying to appear more conservative. The candidates that year generally avoided high-profile ties to labor, feminists, environmentalists and Jewish groups. Michael Dukakis—associated with welfare reform and with making the Massachusetts economy work in the wake of its reputation as Taxachusetts—ran saying that the issue in the campaign was not ideology, but "competence." And, whereas Mondale had picked New York liberal, and woman, Geraldine Ferraro as his running mate, Dukakis picked Texas white guy, non-liberal Lloyd Bentsen.

What was interesting about Lichtman's article in 1982 was, among other things, that it came before Mondale was nominated. At that time, Mondale was the front-runner, but John Glenn—a national hero with a more moderate image—was seen as a real possibility for the Democratic nomination. Also, Lichtman was not making any assumption that Mondale would take his eventual placate-the-interest-groups path to the nomination. Lichtman wasn't making any assumptions one way or the other about who the Democrats would pick or how they would campaign. And yet he was almost ready to call it for Reagan at the height of Reagan's difficulties.

Hmmm.

Back to 1988:

In deploying his keys, Lichtman and co-author Ken DeCell predicted in the May 1988 *Washingtonian* that George Bush would defeat Michael Dukakis.

I'm not sure I can capture here just how out of line that prediction was with what everybody else was saying and thinking from the fall of 1987 through the winter and spring of 1988. Dukakis led in the early polls consistently, sometimes hugely, by 12 to 18 points. The Gallup Poll had him ahead by 16 when the Lichtman prediction came out.

People in the political community often give lip service to the notion that early polls don't mean much. But nobody really means it. If the polls are consistent enough and the margin big enough, people start to see meaning. In this case, the fact that Vice President George Bush was a well-known commodity helped foster the belief that the poll numbers had meaning. He'd been vice president for eight years and had been fairly well known even before that. Apparently the voters had formed their (negative) judgments of him, or so the analysts seemed to think. What could change those judgments at this stage was hard to see.

(This situation was duplicated eerily in late 1999 and early 2000, in an election involving another vice president and another Bush. But the Bush was in a different role. This time George W. Bush—the governor of Texas who, before the campaign, was as unknown to the general public as Dukakis had been as governor of Massachusetts—was in the role that Dukakis had in 1988. Bush the younger was consistently running ahead of Vice President Al Gore in the polls. This caused a spate of articles to be written about Gore's limitations as a politician and a spate of questions about whether Gore should be the Democratic nominee. After all, the voters knew him pretty well, and their opinion of him seemed pretty clear.)

In late 1987 and early 1988, the poll-driven political and journalistic communities bent themselves to the task of explaining what was wrong with Vice President George Bush and the Republicans. *Newsweek* had a poll-driven cover story on Oct. 16 about "The Wimp Factor," a popular buzz phrase in Washington. George H.W. Bush just didn't seem to people like a president; he seemed, in fact, like he was born to be vice president. Everybody was doing that story.

Most commentators took to the task not so much of predicting a Dukakis victory (which is a bigger risk than most want to take), but of explaining it.

Fred Barnes, the knowledgeable conservative writer, was one of the few who had the courage to actually make the prediction. He did a piece in the Feb. 29, 1988 issue of *The New Republic* magazine labeled, "A Donkey's Year: All the Signs Point to a Democratic Victory in November." He said, "I'd bet on (Dick) Gephardt or Michael Dukakis or Albert Gore as probable winners over either of the Republican leaders, George Bush or Bob Dole." He cited liberal writer William Greider of *Rolling Stone* as agreeing with him, and he quoted several leading Republicans expressing pessimism, if not making outright predictions. Barnes' theory—his explanation for Bush's defeat—was that people get tired of having the same party in power and that, although the Republicans had been successful in improving the national economy, the polls showed that people just didn't perceive the success.

In the spring of 1988, I wrote an argument similar to the one Barnes was making. I lectured Lichtman to the effect that—while his approach showed promise—he had left one historical pattern out of his system (a system that was based upon historical patterns). The missing pattern: no party had won the presidency three terms in a row since a constitutional amendment was passed after the Franklin Roosevelt years saying that no person could have the presidency three terms in a row.

I did believe that the good economy in 1988 would help the Republicans. I found Barnes' belief that it wouldn't amazing. I just didn't think it'd be enough.

I wrote, "Bush's big problem is that he's a Republican at the wrong point in the cycle. The rest is mostly noise."

That analysis was not only wrong but wrongheaded. It held that the voters who determine the outcomes of our elections are next to mindless—that they go back and forth between the parties on some sort of schedule—which itself is next to mindless.

That I could be so wrong was particularly remarkable given my recent exposure to enlightenment in the form of Lichtman's predictions about 1984 and 1986.

But poll addiction is a very tough addiction to get under control. Like the other pundits, I wasn't predicting. I was explaining. The polls showed a Dukakis victory, so a Dukakis victory had to be explained.

(Some people made even less sense than I. One local pundit, puzzling over the polls, actually argued that the GOP problem was that times were *too* good. He said the economy was so dynamic that it was causing

42

disruption in people's lives. They found themselves moving to new locations and into new businesses to cash in. That caused them as many problems as it solved. And they blamed the incumbents for the problems.)

By the summer, expectations of a Dukakis victory had become so general that there was no point in making the prediction. The journalists settled for reporting the polls and reporting on what was wrong with Republicans. In conversation, you'd find plenty of people who thought the election would be close—closer than the polls suggested. In fact, most people seemed to think that. But nobody seemed to think Bush would win. And certainly nobody thought he would win easily.

He won easily. He came out of the national conventions ahead, and his lead grew from there.

So what did Lichtman see in the spring that the polls and poll-driven analysts (meaning all the media analysts) did not see?

Lichtman takes more pride in his presidential system than his senatorial system. He says that, applied retroactively, his presidential keys accurately predict the outcome of the popular vote in every election back through 1860, which is to say, really, every election in what might be called the Democratic-Republican era. (The Republicans came into being just before the Civil War.) Moreover—and more than in the Senate schemes—the retroactive "predictions" can generally made with room to spare, so that if there's disagreement about how to turn one or two keys, the prediction stands either way.

In the previous chapter, we saw how the stability of the American two-party system facilitated the development of a system of prediction in Senate elections that is based upon historical precedents. This applies in the presidential realm, too. In many ways, an election in the 1980s looked like an election in the 1880s: the same two parties contesting each other at the same intervals, mostly in the same places.

The presidential prediction scheme has 13 keys. As in the case of the eight Senate keys, there's nothing magic about the number. That's just how many Lichtman found he had to combine to come up with a system that gets every past presidential election right, and does so with room to spare. As a general rule.

He found that the incumbent party has always won the popular vote when no more than five of the 13 keys are turned against it. Again, there's nothing magic about this number. It's just the pattern that developed.

The keys do not predict the Electoral College vote. (In the Electoral College—the official determinant of who takes office—all the votes from any state are officially cast in favor of the candidate who won the popular plurality in that state, even if that plurality was teensy.) This very seldom matters. By 2000, the Electoral College and the popular vote hadn't gone in different directions in 112 years.

In the modern era, the Electoral College outcome actually tends to magnify any margin the popular-vote winner has. The elections of 1960, 1968 and 1976 were paper-thin in the popular vote, but not in the Electoral College. The medium-sized Clinton victories of the 1990s were 2-1 blowouts in the Electoral College. This is because, contrary to what one often hears from political analysts who are pretending they know something that the general public doesn't, a presidential election is not 50 different elections, but one great big one. Trends prevail across much of the country. Many narrow wins in individual states add up to a big win in the Electoral College.

There are exceptions, obviously. And Lichtman does not have a scheme that is correct for every election since the Civil War era at predicting Electoral College outcomes.

The system he did come up with is about how *people* vote. The fact that, once a century, an odd mechanism gets in between the way the people vote and the way an election is decided is not something that such a system can reasonably be expected to deal with.

Below are the keys, along with some commentary (mine, not Lichtman's), and, at the end of each section, a word about how the key was turned in 1988.

As you will see, five of the keys can be said to be about how the country is doing in the election year. A few others are about how the administration and its political party have been faring politically in recent years.

Again, as in the Senate case, none has to do with campaign strategy or the quality of a candidate's campaign organization or the nature of the ad campaigns; none has to do with ideology or the positions a candidate takes on the issues. Almost absent is the matter of a candidate's personality and style. No key mentions "peace"—as in the old "peace and prosperity" theory of what brings incumbent victory. And almost all of the keys can almost always be authoritatively turned—decided— before the campaign actually happens, though not necessarily before the election year.

The keys are phrased as true-false questions, wherein a true favors the incumbent party. Six or more falses, and the incumbent loses.

Key 1 (Party mandate): *After the last midterm elections, the incumbent party holds more seats in the U.S. House of Representatives than it did after the previous midterm elections.*

This is one of the most complicated keys to state, but the concept is simple: either a party is on the upswing over the last two elections or it isn't.

Note that the question is not which party actually controls the House. None of the keys attempts to ascertain which party is the majority party in the country, by any definition. In that sense, the Lichtman scheme is a challenge to a view that's widely held among both scholars and political types: that there are Democratic and Republican eras.

Under the "eras" view, the Republicans were the majority party from the late 19th century to the New Deal, and then again after 1968; the GOP dominated the presidency in those years, and the Democrats in between. This view proceeds from the premise that there must be some reason that one party dominates the presidency during any given era.

Surely, the notion goes, if the only Republican the Democrats lost to between 1932 and 1968 was a great war hero of no particular ideological bent (Dwight Eisenhower), that's another way of saying the Democrats were the majority party. And, surely, if between 1968 and 1992, the only time the Democrats won the presidency was immediately after Watergate, and if their president, Jimmy Carter (also somewhat indistinct ideologically) was unable to win re-election, that tells us that we are talking about an era when the Republicans had a working majority in the presidential electorate.

And surely that suggests that, just as the Republicans were too conservative before 1968, the Democrats were too liberal after.

The Lichtman keys, however, say that both parties are perpetually only one election away from the presidency, depending upon very short-term developments, and that a huge factor in determining which party wins the presidency is how the country is doing during the election year.

This isn't necessarily a complete contradiction of the party-dominance theory. If one party is having difficulty holding the presidency during a given era, that may be because life is more difficult for presidents of the lesser party. That fact can result in election-year circumstances (specified below) that favor the other party.

Still, Lichtman is not saying that party strength is irrelevant, just that the way to look at it is to get a feel for the direction it's going. The first key, standing alone, accurately predicts the outcome of two-thirds of the presidential elections in the last century and a half. That is, if the party with the presidency has gained recently in the House, it has a two-thirds chance of victory in the next presidential election, and if it hasn't it's probably going to lose.

In 1988, the key got a **true** answer, working for Bush. The GOP had gained 17 House seats in the Reagan landslide of 1984 and lost only 5 in 1986.

Key 2 (Contest): *There is no serious contest for the incumbent-party nomination.*

This is the best single predictor of all the keys. By itself, it calls 32 of the past 36 elections. That is, if the incumbent party is pretty much united all along, it wins; if not, it loses, with a few exceptions.

Look at contemporary history: The only three times the incumbent party has been sharply divided at its convention (which is the measure Lichtman uses, rather than votes in primaries), have been 1968, when the Democratic convention city was literally bloody; 1976 when Ronald Reagan was still angling for the nomination at the Republican convention (after a long see-saw primary season against President Gerald Ford); and 1980, when Sen. Ted Kennedy challenged President Jimmy Carter in the primaries then famously failed to shake his hand when they stood together before the convention. Each time, the incumbent party lost.

The most common explanation one hears for this phenomenon is that divisions leave wounds that don't heal by election time, and that some of a party's usual supporters "take a walk," either in the form of not voting, or in the form of not helping in the campaign, or not helping soon enough. This explanation is dubious. The people who feel so passionately about politics as to be furious about a nomination are few in number and are almost certain to vote—for their party. Whether they actually help out in a campaign or contribute financially is probably not terribly important. The same divisions that cause some to sit back cause others to get all the more involved.

Most likely, one reason the second key is so powerful is that internal party divisions reflect widespread public doubts about the performance of the incumbent party. If a presidency is going well—as measured mainly by the country doing well—the party with the presidency is likely to be united behind either the president or the heir apparent.

Another reason the second key is so powerful: Look at the voters who go back and forth between the two parties not only between elections but between various contests on the same ballot. These voters—almost by definition—are not motivated by the ideological disputes that divide the parties. If they preferred one party's world view, they would not be regular swing voters. What the second key suggests is that when these voters see that the case against the incumbent party is made not only by the opposition party, but by many members of the incumbent party, their doubts about the incumbent party increase.

So internal party division not only reflects, but magnifies, public doubts about the incumbents.

In 1988, this key got a **true** response, reflecting well on Bush's chances in the general election. Though a large field entered the early GOP primaries, he locked up the nomination early, and nobody fought him at the convention.

Key 3 (Incumbency): *The incumbent-party candidate is the sitting president.*

Being president is, unmistakably, a credential for being president. This key alone predicts the outcome of more than two-thirds of all presidential elections. Just as in the case of Senate elections, the pattern is not only that the incumbent party tends to win when the incumbent runs; it's that the party tends to lose when he doesn't. As of 1988, the incumbent party had lost three times in the modern era when it had not put up the incumbent president: 1952, 1960 and 1968.

The keys suggest that if a party has a presidency that is not exactly working out—Jimmy Carter's or George H.W. Bush's—the party's best political bet is to stick with it. That way the candidate at least wins this key. If the party tries to dump him, it risks losing the contest key (2), besides the incumbent key (3). And it will probably still get blamed for the problems the nation has (which show up in subsequent keys).

Obviously, in 1988 this key got a **false** answer, a plus for Dukakis.

Key 4 (Third party): *There is no significant third-party or independent campaign.*

Apparently the foment that results in a third party suggests a widespread dissatisfaction with the status quo that bodes ill for the incumbent party. Also, the third candidate may be a way station for disgruntled members of the incumbent party who can't quite bring themselves to vote for an old foe.

The incumbent party lost when Ross Perot ran in 1992, when John Anderson ran as an independent in 1980, and when George Wallace ran on a third ticket in 1968.

But Harry Truman survived when two candidacies split off from the Democrats in 1948, and Bill Clinton survived the less potent Perot challenge of 1996.

In all, this key, standing alone, predicts the outcome of about 70 percent of all presidential elections.

Many Republicans feel that Ross Perot was a bigger problem for them than for Clinton, because he seemed more Republican. Bob Dole tried, in a highly publicized meeting, to get Perot to withdraw from the 1996 race. The keys suggest, however, that Perot was a problem for the Republicans in 1992 and for Clinton in 1996.

To see him as always a greater drain on Republicans requires seeing Perot voters as motivated by what might be called ideological concerns. It requires thinking that they are asking whether the candidate will act in concert with their own values on controversial matters. But, again, voters with strong ideological concerns are probably not the ones who are up for grabs. If a voter wants to see Republican values in the presidency, he's not likely to vote for a non-Republican at the risk of electing a Democrat.

(And, for what it's worth, polls never confirmed the Republican fears about who the Perot voters were. For example, a CNN/*USA Today*/Gallup Poll in late October of 1996 showed 43 percent of Perot voters listing

Clinton as their second choice, and only a third listing Bob Dole. Many said they wouldn't vote at all if not for Perot.)

At any rate, in 1988, there was no significant third-party candidacy. So the answer is **true**. A key for Bush.

Key 5 (Short-term economy): *The economy is not in recession during the election campaign.*

At a certain stage in the 1992 election, five keys seemed to be turned clearly against George Bush. One more, and he would lose. Key 5 was marginal. Even late in the year, it was hard to say whether there had been a recession that year. Just before Labor Day weekend, the government came out with a report saying the economy had lost 200,000 jobs in August. That's when Lichtman turned the key against the incumbent and said his system predicted Clinton victory. The next year, however, the government revised some early conclusions—which it often does—and said 1992 was not such a bad year.

As will be noted in another chapter, Bill Clinton, Al Gore and others associated with the 1992 Clinton campaign were familiar with the keys. Clinton's campaign guy, James Carville, coined the phrase, "It's the economy, stupid." Contrary to a re-write of history that has appeared in much political commentary since, this was not the slogan of the Clinton campaign. Bill Clinton did not go around saying, "It's the economy, stupid." There were no ads saying that. What an amazing slogan that would have been. The line was just graffiti at Clinton headquarters, put there by Carville as an instruction to campaign aides, an answer to the question: What do we emphasize? How do we campaign? Carville was saying that Bush's weakness was the economy, which had been sour for several years.

So the question arises: did Clinton turn the marginal recession key by harping on the down side of the Bush economy? If so, we have a flaw in the keys. A candidate is not supposed to be able to do that. The idea of the keys is that reality is what counts, not political propaganda.

However, if the government itself is reporting a recession that isn't really there, then we are in a nether land between reality and perception. The government's report was important not because all Americans were deeply aware of it directly, but because it helped shape discussion. It shaped how journalists dealt with the economic issues in the campaign. It shaped the hearing Bush got when he tried to paint an optimistic picture. The report itself—at least—was a fact, not a perception.

We shall return two chapters hence to the role of this key in 1992.

At any rate, the recession key is the second most powerful of all the keys, itself predicting the outcome of just over 80 percent of all presidential elections.

In 1988 there was no doubt: no recession. Another **true,** another key for Bush.

Key 6 (Long-term economy): *Real per-capita economic growth during the current presidential term equals or exceeds mean growth during the previous two terms.*

It's not as complicated as it sounds. It's just an effort to measure whether things are moving in the right direction over the long term.

The presence of two keys about the economy makes unmistakably clear that "prosperity" does matter. Chalk one up for conventional wisdom.

A few caveats, however:

From the Lichtman-DeCell book of 1990, *The 13 Keys to the Presidency:* "No (direct) economic gauge whatsoever... is necessary to account for the outcome of any election. Fourteen subsystems (of keys) omit both (economy) keys and still achieve perfect prediction for all 33 presidential contests since 1860." (The smallest subsystem involves only keys one through four, plus seven and thirteen, with the incumbent party needing four.)

So why does the system have 13 keys? It's to make sure that as few calls as possible come down to one key, as noted earlier, but also to increase the chances that the system will continue to be right in future contests.

Meanwhile, of course, the economy is present indirectly in other keys. A bad economy can foment party division, a third-party challenge, even, potentially, social unrest and a loss of congressional seats. Still the ability of the keys to generally work without a direct measure of the economy is worth knowing.

Also worth noting is that the economy keys went in two different directions in four consecutive elections starting in 1972. That suggests that the "prosperity" concept in the "peace and prosperity" cliche is often not very useful in forecasting an election outcome.

Or take 1968: Both economy keys went for the Democrats, and yet the party lost. There were certain problems on the "peace" front. (More about peace below.)

The definition of "prosperity" needs to be focused on. The 1960 election was widely seen at the time as a peace-and-prosperity election. After all, there was no war and no depression. However, both the Lichtman economy keys were turned against Richard Nixon, the candidate of the incumbent Republican Party, who lost. There was a small recession in 1960, and there had been a bigger one in 1958. The 1958 recession was enough to turn the "long-term" key against Nixon.

The 15-year period after World War II is seen in history as a time of extraordinary economic growth that transformed the society from Depression-era poverty to modern suburban affluence. How does that square with Lichtman's portrait of the second Eisenhower administration as economically troubled? The answer is that what Lichtman is measuring in the "long-term economy" key is not prosperity (not, in other words, whether people are doing OK) but, much more specifically, growth in prosperity compared to growth over the previous eight years (not 25 or 30). Eisenhower's second term did see overall economic growth, just not enough.

In 1960, though the Great Depression loomed large in the consciousness of millions of American voters, it apparently wasn't relevant in the election outcome. Presidents seem to be judged by more recent criteria. By its second term, the Eisenhower administration was being compared with its first term and with the years right after the war.

An intriguing British example might be relevant: Margaret Thatcher achieved re-election in part by fostering major progress in the British economy. However, by the time she was ousted after three terms, the economy was widely seen as working against her. It was still much better than it had been under her predecessor, but it was not growing as fast as it had in her own early days in office. That meant trouble.

Theoretically, the long-term economy key could be phrased with no comparison with past times. It could be phrased as the mere absence of depression or recession; it could hold that an average unemployment rate below 5 percent (or some other number) is what counts, or a growth rate above a certain amount. But Lichtman found that a comparison with the growth rate of other recent times is a better predictor. The key, standing alone, predicts the outcomes of about 70 percent of all past presidential elections. That tells us something: the key might be said to be more about economic progress than prosperity. Franklin Roosevelt got the key in 1936, 1940 and 1944. None of those years could reasonably be called good times. But the direction was right.

As for 1988, there was no doubt: the second Reagan term had seen no bad years, unlike both of the previous two presidential terms. The key went **true**, for Bush.

Key 7 (Policy change): *The incumbent administration effects major changes in national policy.*

When, in this and subsequent keys, Lichtman uses the term "major," he means major. The only presidents in the last five decades who have turned this key were Lyndon Johnson, with the civil rights revolution and the war on poverty, and Ronald Reagan, with major tax cuts and a major defense buildup. It's a key that makes life difficult for a president who does not have clear control of Congress.

How the key works can be seen in the 1992 election, when it turned against George Bush and was decisive. He did not control Congress, but, anyway, he was simply a status-quo president, pushing no major agenda. For some presidents in some periods, that is not fatal. But it's a big problem when the country is dissatisfied with the status quo.

In the first years of the administration of the second President Bush, every indication was that the son was trying to avoid the mistakes of the father. Sometimes there's nothing a president can do to make an economy work. But there are other things a president can do to improve his re-election chances. George W. Bush pushed big tax cuts, a newly aggressive foreign policy (from Day One *and* after 9-11), a historic change in Social Security and more. After 9-11, the president at first resisted calls for a Department of Homeland Security, but then got on board. The department had become the symbol of major change in response to the attack, and he apparently liked the idea of major change on his watch.

Senior commentator David Broder called the overall list of George W. Bush proposals a "radical" redirection of the government. But he didn't explain where the radicalism came from. How did the laid-back, down-to-earth, moderate governor of Texas, moderate candidate for president and son of a moderate president become a radical? By watching his father lose an election that he could have won if he didn't have a record suggesting that he was satisfied with the status quo.

Anyway, as for 1988, the policy-change key—which accurately predicts the outcome of just over 70 percent of all elections—did work for Dukakis, through no fault of Vice President Bush. Reagan's second term was not like his first. The answer was **false.**

Key 8 (Social unrest): *There is no sustained social unrest during the term.*

Since 1932 this key has turned against the incumbent only once, in 1968.

And yet this key alone predicts the outcome of two-thirds of all presidential elections. (The key says, if there's no social unrest, go with the incumbent party. If there is social unrest, go with the challenging party. If you follow the key every time, you'll be right two-thirds of the time.)

In 1988, the answer was **true**—there was no social unrest—and the key turned for Bush.

Key 9 (Scandal): *The incumbent administration is untainted by major scandal.*

Lichtman's use of the word untainted is unfortunate, because they all seem to be tainted these days. But the key word is major. The general public must perceive the scandal and be offended by it. Since the historic Teapot Dome scandal in the 1920s—big enough that high-school history students hear about it—only Watergate and the Clinton scandals of 2000 have qualified.

Some might disagree about 2000. After all, the public did not favor removing Clinton from office. But that's a *too*-high standard. The public in general certainly did perceive scandal, unlike in 1996, when Whitewater and other alleged scandals merely raised suspicions. By 2000, the president had lied under oath, and besides carrying on at the White House and lying to the public about it, besides being plagued by other sexual and ethical issues. And the president was impeached, after all.

As for the 1988 election, the Iran-contra scandal of the late Reagan years is somewhat marginal. The offenses seemed extreme to some people, relating to the actual subversion of official government foreign policy. But

Lichtman points out that motivation for the misbehavior—selling arms to Iraq and using the money for anti-communist insurgents in Nicaragua—was ideological, not a matter of serving selfish interests, as in Watergate and the Clinton scandals. Also, the biggest charges didn't lead directly to the president. And the Republicans had succeeded in making Democratic attacks look partisan. Marine Lt. Col. Oliver North had testified on television on behalf of the White House and had scored so well he was being called a "national hero" for a short while.

So the scandal key, which predicts the outcome of two-thirds of all presidential elections, turned in favor of Bush in 1988, with a **true** answer, indicating there was no major scandal. (The key was crucial in determining which way the keys as a whole swung in 1988. There was margin for error.)

Key 10 (Foreign/military failure): *The incumbent administration has suffered no major failure in foreign or military affairs.*

See next key.

Key 11 (Foreign/military success): *The incumbent administration has achieved a major success in foreign or military affairs.*

Keys 10 and 11 are the ones that come closest to measuring the "peace" issue.

They each predict the outcomes of about 70 percent of all presidential elections, with key 11 slightly better than key 10.

Peace itself doesn't work. Abe Lincoln, Franklin Roosevelt and Richard Nixon all got re-elected during war. On the other hand, though, the Democrats lost the presidency during the Korean and Vietnam wars. The pattern is that how the war (or the international situation) is going is more important than whether there is war or peace.

In 1960, there was no war, but both these keys were turned against the Eisenhower administration. The failures were multiple: Cuba had fallen to communists. The Soviets had gotten into space first. A summit collapsed after Ike was found to be lying about a spy incident. And there had been no countervailing advance.

Ironically, at the start of the presidential campaign, it was John Kennedy who was generally seen as having the bigger problem in foreign policy than Nixon. Kennedy's problem was not only that peace prevailed, but that Nixon was seen as more experienced in foreign policy. Nixon had had a very public confrontation with pugnacious Soviet leader Nikita Khruschchev, the very symbol of America's difficulties in the world.

The following is from Kennedy biographer Theodore Sorensen's conventional analysis of the first debate between the candidates.

"Even a draw, if it was a draw, was a Kennedy victory," he wrote. "Shocked Republicans could no longer talk of his immaturity and inexperience.... (Afterward) Nixon talked less of who could stand up to Khruschchev."

Finding a pundit who suggested early on that Nixon was the one with the foreign-policy problem is not easy. However, if you go by the keys, he was. After all, no key measures foreign-policy experience.

In all probability, once a candidate has been chosen by a major political party as its candidate for president, he (or, yes, she) has all the credentials needed to take advantage of the incumbent party's failures.

It should be noted that merely winning a war does not turn a key. In 2000, some might have wondered if the Democrats should be given credit for a major success in military affairs because of the war in Kosovo, which succeeded in taking power over Kosovo from Yugoslavian tyrant Slobodan Milosevic. To turn a key, though, would not be in keeping with the spirit of the keys. The event must result in an improvement in the national situation. Americans clearly don't see the national interest as having much to do with Kosovo.

On the other hand, though, if President Clinton had suffered a humiliating defeat in Kosovo, or had gotten bogged down in a land war, that would have turned the failure key against him. It was a no-win situation, politically.

As for 1988, there was no major failure in foreign policy to turn a key, only historic success: the emergence of the outlines of final victory in the Cold War. The Berlin Wall didn't fall until 1989, under Bush, but real, momentous contention between East and West ended under Reagan on American terms. That was symbolized by Soviet acceptance of a nuclear arms deal in the late 1980s that had been offered by Reagan in the early 1980s.

Key 10 was **true,** and Key 11 was **true,** both foreign policy keys going for Bush.

Key 12 (Incumbent charisma): *The incumbent-party candidate is charismatic or a national hero.*

See next key.

Key 13 (Challenger charisma): *The challenging-party candidate is not charismatic or a national hero.*

Keys 12 and 13 look like a concession to the conventional wisdom about the role of personality in politics. But it's a small concession. The candidacies affected positively by these keys are few: Dwight Eisenhower, John Kennedy and Ronald Reagan are the only modern ones.

Bill Clinton, no; that point is made here because his way with people is often cited as part of the explanation for his political success. No doubt it is. But probably not in general elections. His talent with people is well within the bounds of the ordinary in politics. He never created the kind of movie-star excitement that John Kennedy did, or the kind of emotional attachment that Ronald Reagan did. Indeed, by 1994 the pundits were writing precisely the opposite about him, that what's wrong politically with Bill Clinton is that nobody feels passionately in his favor. Let's remember, too, that we are talking about a president who had exceptionally low poll ratings during the first two years of his presidency.

From an article in *The Philadelphia Inquirer* on Oct. 16, 1994, from the Washington bureau:

"The president's public approval rating has sunk to a new low of 38 percent, according to a national survey released last week by the Times-Mirror Center for People and the Press. Most striking, the poll was taken between Oct. 6 and Oct. 9, when Clinton was at the height of his confrontation with (Iraq's Saddam) Hussein and when his Haiti gamble was looking increasingly like a success.... Clinton remains phenomenally unpopular, and scholars of the presidency say he may be weighted down by factors beyond his ability to change.

"'He seems to evoke some visceral dislike, an antagonism, from so many people,' said George Edwards, director of the Center for Presidential Studies at Texas A&M University. 'It seems to stem less from his performance as a politician or a leader than as a person.'"

When Clinton finally emerged as a popular president in the polls, in the middle of his second term, some conventional pundits tried to find an explanation in his skill as a communicator or his skill with people. But he only achieved consistently high ratings after the evidence was clear that the country was thriving on his watch. That is the explanation for his popularity, not his persona.

Who might pass the "national hero" threshold? Colin Powell? No. True, his poll ratings were astronomical before the 1996 election, when he was talked about as a possible presidential candidate. But he did not have the public standing of Dwight Eisenhower—the last military man in the presidency, a definite national hero. The normal attacks that come along in politics bounced off Ike. They were as nothing in the light of his history of high-profile accomplishment, nothing in the face of the long, loving relationship between him and the people, the likes of which isn't there for Powell.

Even John Glenn never got the "national hero" thing working for him in presidential politics. Maybe he would have if he had survived the primaries, but he got absolutely nowhere in 1984.

Key 12—is the incumbent candidate charismatic?—is enough to predict the outcome of presidential elections only about 60 percent of the time; Key 13, about 70 percent.

In 1998, there was nary a hero or charismatic figure to be found. One **false,** meaning for Dukakis, and one **true,** for Bush.

Counting up the "falses" we get only three, that is, only three factors counting against the incumbent party's candidate, Bush.

The biggest "upset" the keys have ever called—the prediction most in conflict with the prevailing wisdom—wasn't even a close call for the keys.

CHAPTER

6

Making a Believer

Among the conventional analysts, the 1988 election stands as the perfect demonstration that campaigns matter, that the difference between winners and losers is often campaign skill, and that policy issues affect the outcome of general elections. This is because Bush came from behind.

He was losing in the fall of 1987, then through winter and spring, and into the summer. Then he ran a campaign highlighting Michael Dukakis' excessive liberalism. And he won. Proof.

This analysis—in most forms—sees importance in the point that the Bush campaign had seasoned campaign professionals (the Reagan people) whereas the Democrats were starting almost from scratch with the help of only a few losers from past campaigns. The theory holds that the wily old political war horse, George Bush, had been willing to do what was necessary to win, had recognized what was necessary, and had done it, leaving the neophyte in the dust.

Just how sweeping this view of the election was can hardly be captured here. A few examples:

A *New York Times* editorial of Nov. 10, 1988: "Mr. Bush... won because he ran a much more competent campaign and because he fashioned an ideological agenda to which the voters responded."

From a Nov. 14 analysis by John Mashek, of Cox News Service: "In reviewing the GOP nominee's come-from-behind victory over his Republican rivals and then over Gov. Michael S. Dukakis, experience appears likely to have been the most important factor.

"'There's nothing like having been around the track before,' said Lee Atwater, Bush's campaign manager. 'There's not a lot of hard and fast rules. You have to understand the ebb and flow of presidential politics, and he does.'"

If that's the explanation for 1988, then what happened in 1992, when an even more experienced Bush ran against another national neophyte?

Let's call that question rhetorical, for the moment.

In 1988, Bush allegedly struck two chords with the American people that were especially resonant. There was, first of all, the matter of Willie Horton, a black convicted killer who had gotten a weekend release from prison in Massachusetts when Dukakis was governor and had killed again. The furlough policy had been started under Dukakis' moderate Republican predecessor. But the Bush campaign set out aggressively to tie it to Dukakis, who, in fact, defended it.

The second chord was about Dukakis holding that recitation of the Pledge of Allegiance should not be required in the public schools by state fiat.

Bush spent several weeks after the conventions hammering away at one of these issues, then switched to the other. That one-two punch pretty much won it for Bush, the experts decided.

From a *Washington Post* analysis by Thomas B. Edsall and Richard Morin on Nov. 9, 1988: "Bush's victory reflected a successful strategy of holding onto core Republican constituencies... combined with the use of such issues as the death penalty, prison furloughs and the Pledge of Allegiance to win powerful majorities among smaller slices of the electorate."

This analysis has several deep flaws. The main one is, of course, that Lichtman made his prediction of Bush's victory before the campaign.

To any reasonable person, this must raise the possibility that—early polls or no early polls—one need not look to the late-summer and fall campaign for the reasons Bush won. The Lichtman keys "knew" something before anybody knew what strategy Bush would deploy, before anybody had any idea what events would transpire in the campaign.

Nevertheless, the fact that Dukakis had a "lead" and that it vanished must, indeed, be confronted. What happened?

Several factors may have created that lead. Dukakis was shining because he was beating Jesse Jackson, and had yet to come in for the heavy assaults that always materialize in politics eventually. He was emerging unscathed from a crowded field. Meanwhile, Bush was looking small under Reagan's shadow and couldn't emerge until there was a convention celebrating him.

The reasons for the lead don't matter. They were destined to disappear.

As we have seen in discussing 1992, there's a certain point in an election year when it becomes clear to the swing voters that both the candidates are flawed and, yet, respectable and impressive. At that point— the success of the Lichtman keys suggests—the swing voters, instead of attempting to split hairs about which candidate is the most worthy, faces the larger question, the big-picture question: is the current national direction working well enough to be continued?

At that stage, Bush '88 was destined to have the advantage, because the economy was good enough, the international situation was good enough, the domestic scene was peaceful enough, and the Reagan administration was free enough of major scandal.

The notion that Dukakis' problem was excessive liberalism needs to be put up against the fact that Bill Clinton was elected in 1992. They were the same kind of Democrat. Clinton had made the speech nominating Dukakis at the Democratic convention in 1988. They had met as governors and had concluded they were on the same ideological wavelength. Dukakis had one of the earliest welfare reform programs in the country; that was also a pet issue for Clinton.

Then, in the presidential primaries, Dukakis was the one who defeated not only Jesse Jackson, but Illinois Sen. Paul Simon—who was running unabashedly as the traditional liberal Democrat, calling the party to its roots—and Rep. Dick Gephardt, whose major plank was a protectionist stance of the type associated with the Democratic Party's left wing. Dukakis was the guy who wasn't those people.

Yet calling him a liberal "worked" for Bush.

Meanwhile, look at the liberal baggage Bill Clinton carried into 1992: He was the draft dodger, the war protester, the pot smoker and the one with the assertive, feminist wife. He was also the adulterer, which may not exactly be a manifestation of liberal ideology, but in the context at hand did seem to add to the picture of a man whose lifestyle and values were not exactly conservative. Compared to this planeload of baggage, Dukakis' flag and Horton baggage—and his being a "card-carrying member" of the ACLU— look like carry-ons.

Or at least they would have looked that way to the professional explainers of American politics if Dukakis had won and Clinton had lost. That is *totally* predictable.

The political community would have seen the explanation for both elections as obvious: Clinton had a liberal image; Dukakis had a welfare-reformer, problem-solving image, and the Bush effort to change the subject on him to minor, symbolic issues like the Pledge of Allegiance was pathetic.

The pundits would miss the heart of the matter: the year.

If Bill Clinton had been the nominee in 1988, he would have lost. If Michael Dukakis had been the nominee in 1992, he would have won. The difference between 1988 and 1992 was not the difference between Dukakis and Clinton. It was the difference between Bush '88 and Bush '92. In 1988, Bush had no presidential record, only an association with a successful administration. In 1992, though, he was a passive president on whose watch the economy had gone south, the deficit festered, and even Ross Perot started to look good.

The political community believes as one that Dukakis was a bad politician compared to Clinton, that he had, among other faults, no message. His pitch that the election was not about ideology, but competence, is widely derided. But in 1988 there simply was no Democratic message to be had. No critique of the Reagan years would have resonated. Things were just going too well. In 1992, Clinton had the economy and a general sense of governmental impotence going for him; all the factors that fostered the Perot movement. In 1988, Dukakis didn't.

The Clinton campaign was said to be better about responding to campaign charges than the Dukakis campaign had been. A *New York Times* analysis on Nov. 5 by Gwen Ifill was partially labeled, "Sifting Strategies: What Went Wrong and Right." It said, "By anticipating the worst attacks, the Clinton campaign's vaunted 'quick-response team' deflected nearly everything the Republicans threw at them." The same point was made in enough places to eventually become political folklore. But what a strange point it is. After all, the "worst attacks" against Bill Clinton—those noted above: the draft, adultery and all that—were all true and, near as anybody can figure, were generally accepted as true.

Bush certainly had no reluctance about going negative against Clinton in 1992. After all, the strategy had worked in 1988. Toward the end of the '92 campaign, Bush found himself referring to Clinton and Al Gore as "these two bozos."

His problem was not that there was less negative to be said about Clinton than Dukakis. (That is simply absurd.) His problem was that the negative just didn't resonate in 1992.

Bush was in the same position as a candidate in 1992 that Dukakis had been in four years earlier: the big-picture facts spoke for themselves, and political rhetoric didn't matter.

When the Republicans attacked Clinton, they looked as if they wanted to change the subject from Bush's record, which they did. But when they had attacked Dukakis, nobody could make that charge resonate.

The overriding issue in an election is whether the public is open to the idea of change. If it is—as in 1992—it will take a risk on a draft-dodging, adulterous, pot-smoking, war-protesting liberal with a Gloria Steinem-type wife. If it isn't, it will reject the conventional straight-arrow pragmatist—Dukakis—on any charge made against him.

The ideological interpretation of the Dukakis defeat—that he was too liberal, or painted as too liberal—was particularly hard to take seriously for someone who was following the election from Ohio that year. On the ballot was Sen. Howard Metzenbaum, a high-profile, unrepentant liberal. An Associated Press roundup of May 15, 1988, said, "Democrats and Republicans alike say that next to (New Jersey's Frank) Lautenberg, Metzenbaum is the most vulnerable incumbent Democrat, although he seems to be ahead of (George) Voinovich at this stage." This was in keeping with the conventional wisdom of the day, which held that liberalism was a political handicap.

Metzenbaum was to be opposed by the most popular Republican in Ohio, Cleveland Mayor Voinovich, who would be enormously well funded (as would Metzenbaum). And Voinovich was a moderate. So there would be absolutely no question about who had the political center.

Also, Voinovich would eat into the Democratic base: Cleveland. Without a huge win there, Democrats can't carry Ohio.

Also, Metzenbaum was 71 and sometimes seemed to be getting old.

Just in case anybody didn't know about Metzenbaum's liberalism,

Voinovich used his $10 million—in the most expensive campaign to that point in Ohio history—to make it clear. He ran two series of television ads harping on Metzenbaum's alleged refusal to ban child pornography. In other words, he ran the same campaign Bush ran against Dukakis: this guy is a weird, dangerous, out-of-the-mainstream liberal.

Conventional political analysis flatly required that you believe that Metzenbaum was in trouble—even if the Democrats were to carry Ohio in the presidential race, but certainly if they were to lose it big.

But Metzenbaum breezed in, even as pre-season favorite Dukakis got slaughtered in Ohio. Voinovich never got closer in the polls than the 43 percent of the vote he ended up with.

Of course, confronted with the defeat of the more moderate Democrat, Dukakis, and the victory of the more liberal Metzenbaum, the conventional analysts would not admit a serious defeat for the notion that the votes are in the center, or that the liberals were particularly vulnerable in the 1980s. They would point to the advantages of incumbency as the explanation for Metzenbaum's victory. But let's look at the numbers.

Bush's margin in Ohio (14 percentage points) was approximately as big as Metzenbaum's. Do the math and you conclude that about 25 percent of the people who voted for Bush voted for Metzenbaum. (That is, Bush got 57 out of a hundred votes. The Republicans lost 14 of those 57 to Metzenbaum; 14 is about 24.5 percent of 57.)

In other words, 25 percent of the people who voted for Bush—far more than enough to account for his margin of victory—were perfectly willing to vote for a man whose pure liberalism was known to every Ohioan who cared enough about politics to know what liberalism and conservatism are.

Therefore, the widespread belief among political "experts" that the votes of these people for Bush were ideologically motivated is simply amazing.

(There used to be a theory that was deployed to defend this amazing view: that the voters wanted liberals in Congress and a conservative in the White House, because Congress gives out presents, while the president handles foreign policy. It wasn't so much a theory, really, as a desperate effort to hold on to the view that ideology matters in general elections, in the face of the frequent simultaneous elections of liberals and conservatives. By 1988, however, with the anti-communist revolution triumphant in

Russia, foreign policy had, by all accounts, ceased to be a great concern of the American people. After all, by 1992 Bush had solidified his foreign-policy image with a tough approach to the Gulf War, and he still lost that election. As for people wanting a Democratic Congress, tell it to Newt Gingrich.)

To look at the huge and decisive number of people who voted for Bush and Metzenbaum at the same time and say, "Yeah, but Metzenbaum was the incumbent," is hardly responsive to the argument that ideology doesn't affect election outcomes. The fact that he was the incumbent just makes all the more clear that his ideology was known to anybody who cared.

One can argue, of course, that the reason the liberal-bashing strategy "worked" against Dukakis and not against Metzenbaum was that Dukakis was a new quantity, while Metzenbaum was a known quantity. Being unknown, Dukakis was more vulnerable to an attack that defined him in unflattering terms. But, as we have seen, unknownness is only a problem when the public is not looking for change. Clinton in 1992 was just as unknown as Dukakis. But by then the public saw a need for change and was willing to take a chance.

The 1988 election—including Lichtman's success rate in Senate races of roughly 90 percent—was what made a believer out of me.

But problems lay ahead.

CHAPTER

7

Trouble: A Disputed Call in 1992

"Perot is a major threat to the President. Clinton is not."—*Bush pollster Fred Steeper, in an April 28, 1992 memo.*

Although the 1992 election was not particularly close, its outcome was not easy to see until the fall. It wasn't like 1988, when the early polls all went in the same direction for a long time. In 1992, the polls were all over the place.

The outcome was not clear to the political scientists who used statistical methods to make projections. Several of them called a Bush victory, as noted in Chapter 3. It was not clear to journalists. One example of that is below. And it was not clear to Lichtman; an explanation of that is farther below.

Writing a book may not be the most efficient way to convince the public that the "experts" who are in charge of explaining American politics to the American people are befuddled by American politics. The most efficient way would probably be to distribute subscriptions to online databases of old newspaper and magazine articles.

As Chapter 5 noted, Fred Barnes committed a prediction of a Democratic victory in the 1988 presidential election to the pages of *The New Republic* early that year. If he is going to be identified by name, fairness requires reiterating that what separated him from the pack was not his error, but his willingness to go on record with a flat prediction. Remarkably, he was willing again in 1992. (Bless him.) By this time, however, he had learned his lesson. Well, he had learned *a* lesson, anyway.

The lesson he learned was apparently never to underestimate the ability of Republican strategists to find a way to slice up a Democratic candidate for president.

Barnes wrote the May 4, 1992 cover story: "Loser: Why Clinton Can't Win." It needs to be paused over here, not because it is one more mistake, or because there's any point in picking on Barnes. The special value in his piece is that he presented it not merely as his view, but as the view of the insiders, the people in the know. It is a remarkably well researched piece if you consider talking to the insiders to be research, which, of course, by the standard rules, it is. The list of people he quoted and paraphrased as agreeing with him is impressive.

The piece begins, "Vin Weber, the Republican representative from Minnesota, remembers the exact moment he concluded Bill Clinton will never become president." (It was Feb. 6, the day the *Wall Street Journal* printed new evidence that Clinton had dodged the draft, this coming a couple of weeks after a flare-up in the Gennifer Flowers adultery scandal.)

Another passage: "Tubby Harrison, the pollster for Paul Tsongas this year and Michael Dukakis in 1988, has called Clinton 'a dead stone loser' in the fall." In this passage, Barnes notes that loser Dukakis jumped ahead of Vice President George Bush in the polls when he reached the point in the primaries where he clinched the nomination. Clinton didn't.

Another passage on Harrison: "Every party figure he's talked to, the consultant says, 'thinks it's going to be a disaster.' Why? Because Clinton has problems in four separate areas: the character issue, voter turnout, the South, and foreign policy. These problems are all the more troublesome because there's no clear way to overcome them." (On character, Barnes cited four polls making his point that the public had doubts that were not going away. He called the poll numbers "staggering.")

Barnes quotes respected Republican pollster Richard Wirthlin saying, "A candidate can't get on the playing field unless he pays the ticket of honesty and integrity."

And an unidentified "Democratic strategist:" "Once Clinton's negatives are established and allowed to grow deeper and deeper, they're almost impossible to blow away."

Barnes unearths a Clinton problem beyond the usual list: low turnout in the Democratic primaries. He quotes former Sen. Paul Tsongas (a candidate in the early primaries) and then Georgia Secretary of State Max Cleland (later a Democratic U.S. senator), not to mention Bush's Southern coordinator, plus academic turnout expert Curtis Gans on the difficulty that low turnout poses for Clinton. Barnes notes that blacks turned out in smaller numbers in the 1992 primaries than in 1988 (when the Rev. Jesse Jackson was in the race), and says, "I can't imagine how Clinton will lure them in the fall when he couldn't in the spring."

Barnes concludes, "Absent a scandal or economic collapse, Clinton's a goner."

Despite all that, Lichtman's prediction of a Clinton victory was not the kind of against-the-grain prediction the keys made in 1988. Once Clinton took his lead in the polls after the conventions, the conventional wisdom went with him, of course. Still, as Labor Day weekend approached, Lichtman hadn't made any prediction.

Most of the keys could be turned, of course. Key 1 (party mandate) had to be turned against Bush; the Democrats gained a couple of seats in 1988 and a handful more in 1990. Key 2 (contest) had to be turned for the Republicans. Pat Buchanan challenged Bush, but was long gone as a real factor by the convention. Key 3 (incumbency) went for the GOP.

Let's skip over key 4 (third party) for the moment, and key 5 (short-term economy).

Key 6 (long-term economy) was against Bush. The economy's problems in 1990 were the reason Bush came under such pressure to renege on his no-new-taxes pledge: Republican leaders in Congress became convinced that the out-of-control deficit was hurting the economy.

Key 7 (policy change) turned against Bush. Key 8 (social unrest) went for him. Los Angeles had had a major riot, but the causes were local, and other riots didn't occur. Key 9 (scandal) also turned for Bush. There was nothing major.

Both foreign-policy keys—numbers 10 and 11, about a failure and a success, respectively, turned for Bush. There was no failure, and the Gulf War was a success. True, Bush's astronomical post-war poll ratings came down so fast that some people concluded that, by late 1992, the war was simply forgotten by the public. Moreover, Bush was coming in for growing criticism for not having used the opportunity of the war to get rid of Iraqi leader Saddam Hussein. But the war was an enormous event at time. American interests (in the free flow of oil) were unmistakably seen as directly at stake, not to mention the presence of hundreds of thousands of Americans in harm's way. And the outcome, from that perspective, was a clear victory, with Iraq having to withdraw from Kuwait, and with U.S. casualties very low. Those have to be considered the issues the public really cared about, not whether Saddam stayed in office.

Indeed, if Bush had been governing with an eye on the keys, he would have done exactly what he did in the Gulf: moved ahead with war before exhausting all diplomatic options.

To some people whom Republicans respected—including Chairman of the Joint Chiefs of Staff Colin Powell and Sen. Sam Nunn—it seemed that Bush moved prematurely. Nunn said war ought to be a last resort. He wasn't questioning whether Saddam—who had invaded oil-rich Kuwait unprovoked—had to be removed from Kuwait. But some people felt that Saddam had blundered into his move partly because he had misinterpreted American intentions. Indications had arisen that Saddam might be looking for some face-saving way out.

By this time, however, American troops had been in Saudi Arabia, on the Kuwait border, for months. If it became many more months, with the beginning of the long, modern election season not very far off, this could start to look like a setback for the United States. And a negotiated settlement could look like something less than a victory.

If you are playing to the keys, you move in fast and hard and get the thing resolved.

This is not to say that Bush played to the keys. I have no information on that. It is known that Lee Atwater, a key Bush political adviser, was familiar with the keys. The 1990 Lichtman-DeCell book has a blurb from him: "As far as I'm concerned Lichtman and DeCell are geniuses. The Thirteen Keys to the Presidency are almost infallible. They were predicting a Bush victory (in 1988) back when no one thought he had a chance." Atwater devoted a page of his own book to the keys.

But the truth is, you don't have to know about the keys to be politically afraid of getting bogged down in some foreign deployment. The don't-get-bogged-down ethic grows out of the Vietnam experience, which was still affecting foreign policy in the early 1990s.

Back to the list of keys: The final two keys—about charisma and hero standing—split between the two parties. Neither party had a loved or revered candidate.

So, leaving out the third-party and recession keys, we see four keys having "false" answers and turning against Bush (the incumbent party's standing in the House; the long-term economy; policy change, and incumbent charisma).

Both the unresolved keys—key 3 (third party) and key 4 (short-term economy)—had to turn against Bush for him to be predicted to lose. There had to be a significant third party and an election year recession.

Co-Authors Split

I have left the two keys unresolved until now because Lichtman and his co-author Ken DeCell split over how to turn them, and they require more comment.

The disagreement itself was something of a crisis for the system. Lichtman had always insisted that, though the keys might look somewhat subjective in nature—might look like matters of judgment—reasonable and informed people would almost always turn them the same way, once they understood the system and had looked at how the keys had been turned in previous races. Whether that's true is an important question, because if the subjectivity level is high enough, the system has no real value.

Well, DeCell is certainly reasonable and informed. He's not a historian, like Lichtman, but a journalist. However, Lichtman never said you have to be an historian to know how to turn the keys.

Another reason 1992 is important to pause over is that Lichtman had presented his system as one that predicts outcomes with room to spare. Typically, when incumbents have lost, they've had not six keys turned against them, but eight. Before 1992, only one incumbent loser had six: Benjamin Harrison, when he lost to Grover Cleveland in 1892. And typically when incumbents won, they had only three or fewer keys turned against them. Only Harry Truman in 1948 and Grover Cleveland in 1888 (the year when he won the popular vote—and the keys—but lost the Electoral College) had the marginal five.

Keeping in mind that 1992 was only the third presidential election in which the keys were deployed *before* the election, rather than in retrospect, this issue arose: if it turned out that the keys that produce clear-cut calls in past elections produce a lot of marginal calls in future elections, that's a flaw in the system.

The goal is clear-cut calls, as well as easily called keys.

As it turned out, though, the 1996 election—which the keys called correctly—was another one-key election, though without disputed calls. That is, five turned against the incumbent; one more, and the call would have gone to Dole. The 2000 election was another one-key call.

Lichtman and DeCell had been making a habit of putting their predictions in a pre-election issue of *Washingtonian* magazine, where DeCell was an editor. The earlier they could make the predictions, the happier they were. In 1988, the presidential call was made in the spring. In 1992, that wasn't possible.

Finally DeCell went ahead, without Lichtman, with a piece in the September edition, sent to press near the beginning of August.

DeCell called both keys in favor of Bush, saying, in other words, that there was no significant third party and no election-year recession.

He concluded, "Barring a combination of negative developments—sudden economic downturn, an outbreak of widespread civil disorder, or a disastrous setback in foreign affairs—George Bush will be re-elected on Nov. 3."

Let's look at the two keys:

The reason DeCell didn't consider Ross Perot a significant enough factor to turn the third-party key against Bush was that Perot had pulled out of the race when DeCell was writing. He wrote:

"The aborted Perot campaign, unprecedented in election history, obscures the call somewhat on key 4. Perot's brief bid was significant while it lasted, and it clearly (reflected) discontent within the country; with the candidate's name still on the ballot in many states, an argument can be made that key 4 should be turned against the GOP. But with Perot himself having dropped out of the race even before the major-party candidates were formally nominated, a 'strict constructionist' call turns key 4 back in the GOP's favor."

In the Lichtman-DeCell book (the Bible), key 4 reads, "There is no significant third-party or independent campaign." The authors define the key this way, in part: "For upcoming elections, any candidate who appears likely to win 5 percent or more of the popular vote is a 'major' third-party contender."

The surrounding text makes clear that the point of the key is that the emergence of a new, major third party is a measure of the kind of discontent that spells trouble for the incumbents.

Lichtman, who made his call at Labor Day, called both keys against Bush, seeing both a significant third party and a recession.

In the October *Washingtonian,* he wrote, about key 4 (third party): "Insurgent campaigns count against incumbent parties in part because they are barometers of discontent. Ross Perot's withdrawal has not quieted the discontent or ended his campaign. He is spending millions of dollars to keep his state-level operations going and will be on about 45 state ballots. In some polls, Perot still scores about 15 percent—better than John Anderson, the last insurgent candidate to turn the key, at a comparable point in 1980. The Perot phenomenon could disappear by November, but it hasn't yet." Lichtman turned the key against Bush.

The disagreement is, in one sense, moot, because Perot re-entered the race, and got about 20 percent of the vote. That resolved the dispute about whether his candidacy was major. But it did not end the dispute about what call should have been made in the summer. That, after all, is the important question. We are talking about a predictive scheme here, not just another after-the-fact analysis.

Underlying the split between the co-authors was something more than a difference of opinion. DeCell didn't relish going with the new conventional wisdom. Because of the polls showing Clinton ahead, the talk in the media had quickly changed from what a flawed candidate Clinton was to what a wonderful campaign organization he had. The aforementioned "quick-response team" was being lionized. DeCell—one could tell—was wondering whether Lichtman was trying to read the keys in a way that comported with a gut feeling that Clinton was going to win. The issue was intellectual honesty.

My view is that Lichtman's reading of the third-party key cannot be faulted. DeCell is intellectually honest in noting that he was deploying a "strict constructionist" reading of the keys, and in noting that others might disagree. He felt justified in adopting the strict standard because Lichtman had promulgated the general rule that turning the keys should be difficult, that "major" meant "major," that not just anything (not, in this case, an aborted campaign) could turn a key. But applying a strict constructionist reading to such an odd set of developments as prevailed in the Perot situation—he's in; he's out; he's in—can cause one to lose the essence of the situation. The old legal maxim "Tough cases make bad law" applies here. To expect a predictive scheme that is based upon historical precedent to deal smoothly with the erratic, singular likes of Ross Perot is to expect too much.

The recession key is more problematic. DeCell wrote in August: "This election-year economy has no clear historical antecedent.... With continued high unemployment and sluggish consumer demand, the current recovery still feels like a recession to many people. But the broadest gauge of economic performance indicates that the economy has been growing, however fitfully, for the past five quarters. The first quarter of this year saw real annualized growth in gross domestic product of 2.9 percent—almost double the 1.5-percent average of the first three years of Bush's term. The growth rate slowed to 1.4 percent—almost flat per-capita—for the second quarter. Still, that's not a recession. Unless the economy turns noticeably downward in the third quarter, key 5 remains in the Republicans' column."

Lichtman rebutted in September: "The short-term-economy key depends on the economy's last major turn, not on the technical definition of a recession. We turned it against the incumbent parties in 1960 and 1980 without a formally defined recession (two consecutive no-growth quarters); doing otherwise would have contradicted both the economic and the political realities of those elections.

"Continued weakness," he wrote, "including disappointing employment numbers in the latest report (at Labor Day), indicates that the economy has not yet made the upturn needed to put the recession behind us."

Who was right? In their 1990 book, Lichtman and DeCell wrote the key as, "The economy is not in recession during the election campaign." However, the book does make clear that the word recession is not used in the technical, two-quarters sense. Instead, the emphasis is, indeed, on the last "change in direction" of the economy. Lichtman saw the last change in 1992 as being the drop in growth from the first quarter to the second.

That, in itself, is not compelling. Surely a drop from 6 percent to 4 percent would not be considered a "recession" by any definition, technical or not. Moreover, changes in direction are sometimes hard to perceive until all the data are in, months too late.

Lichtman eventually came out with a new, smaller version of the 1990 book, *The Keys to the White House, 1996.* In it, he phrases the key the same way—is there an election-year recession—but he abandons the last-turn standard. Instead, he turns the key "if the overwhelming public perception is one of an economy in recession... even if the economic statistics might suggest a more ambiguous situation."

The revised standard is disappointing to us enthusiasts. To consider public opinion is to take a step away from a central claim for the keys: that they measure reality, not appearance. Meanwhile, one has to wonder about our ability to measure public opinion in the races of the 19th century (or, for that matter, to know when the economy changed its direction in that era). Successful retroactive "predictions" about those races are part of the case for attention to the Lichtman scheme.

Lichtman is not giving full authority to the public, just authority in an "ambiguous" situation. The possibility of an ambiguous situation prevailing with regard to a decisive key is small. Still, I'd be happier with a more concrete measure.

Now, obviously, public opinion is present in other keys. Says Lichtman, "Scandals reach the threshold needed to topple key 9 only when there is bipartisan recognition of the problems besetting an administration." "Recognition" is some sort of reference to public opinion.

Moreover, one possibility worth entertaining seriously is simply that the public was right and the statisticians were wrong. The statisticians often revise their formulas and such. That suggests that they know that problems set in with their methodology. I found as I distributed early versions of this book that some level-headed people (from different parts of the country) remembered 1992 as bad times and found Bush's insistence to the contrary to be other-worldly.

At any rate, the concession Lichtman has made is one he would rather not have to.

DeCell and Lichtman are not exactly buddies these days, but DeCell is still an enthusiastic advocate for the keys. He also thinks, however, that some races may just be too close to call by the keys. He puts 1992 in that category.

In an interview in 2000, he noted that when Lichtman first proposed a presidential scheme, it entailed a middle range where no call could be made. If five of the 13 keys were turned against the incumbent, there would be no call. Under that system, the 1912 election was a five-key race that could not be called in retrospect; it was the only such election. Then a reader offered Lichtman a way to eliminate that mid-range. That is, Lichtman tweaked the system and came up with a way to make a successful after-the-fact prediction about all the races back to the Civil War era. That's the system now in use.

DeCell is right in suggesting that the keys don't have to be able to predict the outcome of every election to provide the best framework we have for understanding politics, or at least a much better one than the prevailing one.

Eternal Perfection Not the Claim

The difficulties of 1992 seem less important now than they did then. Of the six presidential elections in which the keys have been used prospectively, only 1992 proved very troublesome in predicting the popular vote. That's good enough.

Lichtman himself is quick to say the presidential keys won't be right every time. The Senate keys aren't, after all. The point has never been perfection. He seems to me less interested in perfection than in having a system that is better than the other academic predictive schemes.

The subjectivity of the keys is the main case the political scientists make against Lichtman, the historian. Our numbers are hard; his judgments are soft, they say. In *Before the Vote*, James E. Campbell's and James C. Garand's aforementioned book on the statistics-based predictive schemes, the authors say, "It is tempting to criticize... Lichtman's keys for the subjectivity and crudeness of (the) indicators, as well as... how they are combined to predict simply a winner or loser (rather than the candidate's portion of the vote)."

Only to academics is there a more important question than who wins and who loses.

Every predictive scheme has its drawbacks, and subjectivity is Lichtman's. But, really, the subjectivity is minimal, once you understand how the keys have been turned in the past, once you get a feel for what the standards are. You come to know that, in talking about foreign failures and successes, or scandals, or policy change, we are not talking about the sorts of ups and downs, successes and failures that happen in any administration. There has to be something special.

The Senate keys are even less subjective.

Still, gushing as this book is about the "predict-ability" of the keys, the fact is the 1990s had a sobering effect on us zealots. The reason DeCell went ahead and called the 1992 election in August was that the magazine was on record with the judgment that races can be called early. The reason it was on record was that past elections always seemed—judging from the history of the keys—to be callable six months before November.

Turns out, that isn't always the case.

Of course, one reason most past races look callable early is that the retroactive predictions have a key or two to spare.

Turns out, that's not always the case, either, in real time.

It also turns out that presidential elections are not the only ones that can sober up us zealots a little. More on that in due course.

While we're on the subject of the peculiarly problematic presidential election, 1992, one other question remains to be asked. It was referred to in Chapter 5: Did the Democrats make the recession key work for them by harping on how awful the economy was? Did they turn the key by influencing public opinion (which Lichtman now acknowledges to be crucial)?

The question can't be answered concretely. What's known is that some important people have been familiar with the keys for a long time.

By the late 1990s, the keys were fairly well known to a large number of political players in Washington. Lichtman had appeared with some frequency on both local and national television. Articles had been written about his system at every presidential election for a decade. He actually appeared with Carville on C-SPAN. Carville affectionately—or something—called him "professor."

In the early 1990s, the keys system was not so well known. However, when Arkansas Gov. Bill Clinton was asked on television after the Gulf

War whether he was going to run for president—given that no other Democrat seemed to want to—he responded with a list of factors that determine whether a president is vulnerable: party unity, the economy, a foreign-policy success, domestic tranquility, policy change, etc. To the initiated, it was obvious that he had the keys on his mind. Clinton is said to have read the 1990 book eagerly, to the point of underlining what he saw as key passages. Al Gore, too, is thoroughly familiar with the keys.

One might suggest that Carville and Clinton didn't need the "professor" to tell them the importance of the economy. This was one case, after all, where the folk wisdom of politics and this other form of wisdom could come together to the same conclusion. Even if you believe, as Lichtman strongly does, that the economy is not the be-all-and-end-all of presidential politics, one might ask what else the Democrats were supposed to run on in 1992? Character? Foreign policy?

But that question itself seems to arise out of a keys-influenced state of mind. After all, Democrats could have decided to simply run on the differences between the Democratic world view and the Republican one. They could have settled for emphasizing the more popular parts of the Democrats' perspective and downplaying or modifying the other parts. That would be a fairly conventional approach.

However the Democrats got to their strategy, the question remains: Suppose everybody knew about the keys and their record. Suppose everybody believed. How would that affect the behavior of candidates? And if the candidates behave in a certain way, will they be able to screw up the predict-ability of the keys? It is a question we will reach in the final chapter.

The details on 1996: As noted above, though the prediction of a Clinton victory was close—resting on one key—none of the calls on the individual keys were close. Whitewater never passed the basic threshold to be considered a major scandal: bipartisan agreement that there was a major scandal. There was no major foreign-policy failure that was anyplace near the size of events that had turned that key in the past. The Los Angeles riot didn't spark national unrest. Bob Dole was not charismatic. The long-term and short-term economies were both strong.

The keys Clinton lost: seats in the House (what with the GOP takeover in 1994); a major third party, what with Perot getting about 10 percent of the popular vote; the absence of a major change in national direction, what with welfare reform not being big enough and being perhaps more a congressional initiative than a Clinton one; absence of a major foreign-policy success; and Clinton not being charismatic on the order of Reagan, Kennedy or FDR.

In case you're curious, our friend Fred Barnes didn't write a major magazine piece predicting the outcome of the race. (Finally, a lesson learned?) He did write in the March 25 *Weekly Standard*—a conservative publication—that the Clinton people were repeating the 1992 mistakes of the Bush people: not taking the opposition seriously enough. Barnes reported that he found the Democrats ridiculing Bob Dole as an inept, weak candidate, just as the Republicans ridiculed Bill Clinton. He leaves out that he found the ridicule of Clinton appropriate enough at the time to form the base of his predictive article. But he should be forgiven for that, because after the 1996 election he wrote that Clinton's re-election was "inevitable." He acknowledged that this wasn't always clear to everyone in politics. And he cites, at length, as his major source for his conclusion of inevitability—are you ready?—Allan Lichtman. Progress.

CHAPTER

8

Trouble II: Everybody Misses 1994

We're not going to look in detail at all elections after 1992, but 1994 must be paused over. It confounded both Lichtman and the conventional analysts.

It was, of course, the historic Republican tidal wave. The party gained control of the House of Representatives for the first time since the early 1950s. It gained 54 seats from its level after 1992, bringing it to 18 more than a majority. Everybody knew before the election that the party was going to gain seats; some people thought it might take control. Nobody foresaw the size of the victory except Newt Gingrich, and nobody paid him much attention because he *always* seemed to see a Republican tidal wave coming.

Meanwhile, the Republicans in the Senate went from 43 after 1992 to 53, winning control with, again, more seats to spare than was generally anticipated. Lichtman hadn't predicted major gains. The Republicans made similar gains in state government, taking a majority of governorships and a huge majority of big-state governorships. Never in anybody's memory had a party made such a wide variety of such impressive gains.

(Lichtman's only prediction schemes are for the Senate and the presidency. By the time he had developed and tested them, in the 1980s, the House hardly seemed worth focusing on, because incumbents were winning well over 90 percent of the races in which they ran. A one-key scheme would not have generated much interest. As for governorships, Lichtman did look at them enough to conclude that they have a different dynamic from presidential elections. They do not depend clearly on how things are going for the state.)

The tidal wave did not seem to figure. When you look at past years in which enormous changes took place in the House, the reasons are obvious: bad times or big scandals. But in 1994, the country was prosperous and peaceful. The Clinton scandals were not huge. (They didn't seem to matter two years later.)

Was the problem Bill Clinton's relatively low poll ratings? Well, Ronald Reagan was at the peak of his popularity when he lost control of the Senate in 1986, and Republican President Dwight Eisenhower was popular when the Democrats had a huge year in the Senate in 1958.

So what was it about 1994? The Republicans claimed an ideological victory, an endorsement of their conservative "Contract with America," and a rejection of Bill Clinton's liberal path. It was true, after all, that Clinton was finding himself on the wrong side of the public opinion polls every time he turned around. He proposed a tax increase. He pushed for free trade. He was associated with the cause of gays-in-the-military. He pushed a plan for universal health care, which seemed a popular idea at the beginning of the debate, but not at the end. Meanwhile, he had set aside for later consideration the not-so-liberal part of his election platform: welfare reform.

In the campaign, the Republicans were focused and consistent. They ran against big government. The Democrats were unfocused and wavering. Most tried to distance themselves from the president, running completely on local issues and their own records. Late in the campaign, the White House and the party started making a national case for Clinton, but it was, at best, too little, too late.

One race encapsulates the nature of the year: the Speaker of the House lost a re-election bid. Tom Foley had been elected and re-elected and re-re-elected in his Spokane, Wash., district for decades, partly because he was a rising force within the Democratic Party. Districts take pride in representatives who achieve national recognition. Independent voters see such success as a resolution of all doubts about who is "the better man" in a particular contest. Speakers do not lose re-election bids.

And Tom Foley's opponent was no fireball. George Nethercutt had run three times before without success. When he got to Congress, he went nowhere. In 1994, he was simply the un-Foley. The man who wasn't a local institution won because he wasn't a Democrat.

Nationally, the notion that the people had voted for "less government" was bipartisan in its acceptance. Former Dukakis aide Susan Estrich wrote in the *Los Angeles Times,* "If there was an affirmative agenda to come out of Tuesday's vote, it was the demand for less government." One non-partisan analyst wrote in that paper that if campaign rhetoric means anything at all in election outcomes, the voters certainly had voted for less government.

But the possibility that campaign rhetoric *doesn't* mean anything shouldn't be dismissed out of hand. After all, the very people who were newly elected in 1994 on the anti-government pitch were in widespread disrepute less than a year later, having pursued their agenda aggressively, to the point of shutting down the government. The Democrats regained the political initiative. They held their own for several years after that, though every new Clinton State of the Union speech offered a bevy of active-government initiatives. True, Clinton—accepting the conventional interpretation of the election—declared the era of big government over. And the Democrats stopped pushing anything so big-government as universal health care. But they pushed gun control, campaign finance controls, HMO regulation, mandatory V-chips (for violence) in televisions and much more.

By 2000, the Republicans had decided to fight for the political center, rather than raise the anti-government flag. They rallied—no-questions-asked—around "compassionate conservative" George W. Bush for the 2000 presidential election, and, once they did so, he moved even closer to the center. The era of smaller government died about a day and a half after the era of big government.

The notion that the 1994 election was a call for less government is as dubious as the notion that the 1992 election was a call for more government. Few people ever articulated that interpretation of 1992. But President Clinton—whose party solidly controlled both houses of Congress—proceeded in his first two years as if he thought he had a traditional liberal mandate, what with his call for higher taxes and universal health care.

Therein lies the interpretation of 1994 that I adopted. What was different about that year from other midterm elections was that one party controlled the White House and both houses of Congress and was proceeding on an activist, ideological path that was giving the other party fits.

The last time one party had gone into a midterm election controlling everything was 1978. But Jimmy Carter did not have the kind of focused, programmatic agenda that Clinton had; his midterm losses were more modest (15 in the House).

The time before that was 1966, when the Democrats lost 47 seats in the House. They had been pursuing an agenda so aggressive as to make Clinton look passive. (The other difference between President Lyndon Johnson and Clinton was that Johnson had been successful in enacting his agenda; Clinton showed that legislative success is not a prerequisite for midterm failure.)

The time before that was 1954, when Republicans had control of everything, but only marginally in both houses. Those Republicans were not nearly such activists. But their losses were small; it just so happened that small losses were enough to change control of Congress.

If you go back to 1934, you can find a midterm election in which one activist party controlled everything and still made gains. But that was a time when the country saw no hazard in change, because the status quo was so bad. Times have never been nearly so bad since.

These days, I concluded, if one party is screaming bloody murder about the other party's agenda—whether it's the Republicans screaming about universal health care or the Democrats screaming about the Contract with America—the activist party has a problem.

This is not to say that change is unpopular. Welfare reform was certainly popular. What's shunned is bitterly contested change that seems to be of a partisan type.

In good times, the party that reminds people that things could be worse—and that policy changes might make them worse—is in a good position.

My interpretation of the 1994 election as a vote against activist, one-party government looks somewhat undermined by Republican successes at the state level, where the election actually created cases of one-party dominance. But, after all, the state elections didn't confirm the anti-government interpretation of the election either; most of the popular Republican governors and candidates for governor of the era—George W.

Bush, George Voinovich in Ohio, two different Republicans in Illinois, and more—were problem-solving centrists, rather than anti-government crusaders. The public doesn't seem to fear one-party government like that.

Another problem for my interpretation of 1994 arose in 2002. George W. Bush was a lot like Clinton in that year: a president elected with a minority of the popular vote who adopted an agenda that was aggressive enough to set off the other party. He pushed for tax cuts, public support for faith-based community groups, a new missile-defense system, and a generally more contentious, unilateral approach to foreign policy. He spoke of revamping Social Security in a conservative direction. He pushed for highly controversial judicial appointments. Liberals and conservatives alike were seeing a return to the conservative glory days of the first half of Ronald Reagan's first term.

There was no backlash against Bush. Unlike both Clinton and Reagan, he presided over midterm gains in both the House and Senate for his party. The Republicans regained control of the Senate, having lost it between elections, when Vermont Sen. Jim Jeffords left the party. The Republican gains in the House were the first since 1994 and the first any president had seen in his first term since 1934.

Why did Bush do so well compared to Clinton? Well, 9-11 probably figures in someplace. It had happened a year before the 2002 campaign, and it dominated everything. For one thing, it pretty much brought Bush's domestic legislative pursuits to a halt.

So maybe *just* ticking off the other party isn't necessarily enough.

My theory has not been cleared with Lichtman. He might not accept it. But it is Lichtmanesque in the sense that it does not focus on the campaign as an explanation for the outcome of the election, but on pre-existing circumstances.

Perhaps, however, it tries too hard to uphold Lichtmanism. Maybe the best way to see 1994 is simply as an exception to the rule that campaigns don't determine outcomes. Maybe the year should be acknowledged as so unusual as to mess up any analyst who thinks in terms of historical precedents.

Every election has *something* new, or something that, at least, seems new. Typically, however, it's not nearly enough to matter. But this election had, for starters, Newt Gingrich, in his full flowering.

Gingrich had been building an effort to take over the House of Representatives for years. He had relentlessly worked on every aspect of the task, from highlighting issues to finding candidates to funding them. By 1994, he had failed in a string of elections. He had failed even to make progress toward the goal. So it was becoming increasingly tempting to ignore him. But in 1994 almost everything came together for him.

Though the country was not doing badly under the Democrats, every policy change they had become associated with—taxes, health care, gays, trade—was unpopular enough that they consistently found themselves changing the subject from policy matters. That unpopularity was an extraordinary thing, perhaps more extraordinary than Gingrich. Typically, democratic governments like to do *popular* things.

And typically the change-the-subject impulse takes hold of an incumbent party only when times are bad. In those cases, the election goes to the other party, and some analysts mistakenly see the incumbents' campaign as the reason, though it is really only the symptom of their problem.

But in 1994 the Democrats' absence of anything to say on the issues contrasted extraordinarily sharply with the clear purposefulness, the energy, the sense of direction of the Republicans. That sense of direction was founded partly in Gingrich's architectural work but also in Republican certitude in the party's rejection of the Clinton agenda.

In this rare case, perhaps, the campaign mattered, not merely as the usual refraction of the circumstances prevailing in the country or in individual states, but as a force in itself.

An Amazing Kind of Error

Let's look at how the conventional analysts handled 1994 as it was developing. The shape of their failure commands attention.

It is, indeed, a classic in the annals of failure. In a year when Republican strength was showing up almost everyplace, the conventional analysts not only failed to see the national wave coming; while missing it, they actually managed to see Republican strength in the few cases where it turned out not to exist.

The sheer unlikeliness of that must be paused over. If the pundits see a particular Republican as especially promising even as Republicans go, and if that Republican manages to lose while all the run-of-the-mill (or worse) Republicans are romping to victory all across the country, often by historic margins, then the pundits are not simply wrong, but fascinatingly wrong. What could possibly account for their *total* cluelessness? Could people selected randomly off the streets be any more wrong than the people whose job it was to explain American politics to the American people?

Immediately before the election, the media did know it would be bad for the Democrats. Give them that much. But it's not much. They had late polls, which tend to be pretty good, even if early ones aren't. And, after all, midterm elections were always assumed to be bad for the party that holds the presidency.

But let's focus on the question of just how bad the media thought it would be. In late October, what the media found happening when they surveyed the political scene was a Democratic surge. Typical was a *Christian Science Monitor* piece on Nov. 1: "Races for Congress Tighten Across US As Democrats Attack."

Said CBS on Oct. 30: "Elections (are) Just Nine Days Away and Surveys Show Democrats Battling Back." *Boston Globe* columnist David Nyhan, writing on the same day, was the extreme case, positively gloating about the dashing of the GOP's earlier confident predictions: "The Democratic voters who were disappointed in Clinton, worried about the economy and furious at Congress, those Democrats, are coming back," he insisted.

In general, where the media were most unguarded was in discussion of particular races. And what they had to say about some of them is what's most striking. Classic was a piece in the *Evening Standard* of London, clearly taking a cue from what the American media were saying (as documented below). In a Nov. 8 story about the troubled campaigns of the Senate Democrats seeking re-election, the *Standard* cited only three examples: Ted Kennedy; Dianne Feinstein, and Chuck Robb.

They all won.

Let's look at these three races and how the media handled them:

Massachusetts

In 1994, if you wanted to maintain official standing as a member of the media elite, you were required to write or speak the following words at least three times:

"Ted Kennedy is in the fight of his life."

A search of computer archives shows that the fight-of-his-life mantra appeared in the local media (in the *Boston Globe* and the *Herald;* in the latter it was used at one time or another by nearly every member of the staff). It was also in the national media (*Newsweek,* CNN); the international media (*The Economist* and the London *Evening Standard*); and the outerspace media (The McLaughlin Group television shout show, on at least two consecutive weeks, by two different participants). The phrase was used by some of the most respected pundits: Howard Fineman of *Newsweek,* and Morton Kondracke of television and other media, and in the headline of a piece by Ronald Brownstein of the *Los Angeles Times*. And this list is just fragmentary.

Now, to say that the race was the toughest of Kennedy's life was, admittedly, not to say that he would lose. (The *Globe*'s Ellen Goodman, however, did say "defeat is in the air.") But it is certainly to say the race would be close, at least in the absence of some extraordinary scandal hitting Kennedy's opponent. Well, there was no such scandal.

And the race wasn't close. It came out 58 to 41 in percentages. By common consent of the punditry corps, that's near landslide territory.

(In his first election, Kennedy won by only 55-42. And in two re-elections he had received roughly comparable 61 and 63 percents.)

The punditry corps went wrong in the classic way: looking at the early polls. The polls seemed to confirm common sense. The pundits saw a liberal running against a moderate, and they thought it was obvious the moderate had the advantage on ideology. They saw a young, trim man (Mitt Romney) running against a bloated sexagenarian whose appearance seemed a metaphor for his out-of-date views. They operated—as always—from the premise that imagery is of fundamental importance, and they simply knew that young, trim and cool is better than old, fat and hot.

They saw, too, that this was one time when Kennedy didn't have a monumental advantage in money, because his opponent was wealthy.

And they operated—as always—on the premise that the only thing more important than imagery is the money necessary to manipulate images.

To them, it was clear that, if all these factors did not add up to the inevitability that Romney would defeat Kennedy, they certainly meant that he would give him the fight of his life. The analysts thought that in using that phrase they were taking no risk. They are generally loath to take risks. They thought it was obvious.

If you accept the basic premises of modern political punditry, it *was* obvious.

California

"If Republicans are to regain control of the Senate this fall, it will be at least partly because of the free-spending ways of Michael Huffington."

When Thomas D. Elias, of Scripps Howard News Service, began his early October analysis of the California senatorial election of 1994 with that statement, he surely did not mean to be making a bold and risky prediction; that's not the idea in an analysis that runs in the news pages (as opposed to some editorial-page pieces). He was—just by way of emphasizing the importance of Huffington's money—making a statement he thought could not reasonably be disputed. The notion that, in an exceptional Republican year, their most fantastically funded candidate might lose—when the polls were looking good—didn't seem to make sense.

As Elias reported, journalists were not alone in seeing things this way: "Republicans feel they need to take (the California) seat to reach a Senate majority."

It was apparently the polls that caused Lou Cannon—as sophisticated an analyst as journalism offers—to write in the Sept. 28 *Washington Post,* "(T)he great mystery man and big surprise of the 1994 election campaign is Republican Michael Huffington, who seems well on the way to buying himself a seat in the Senate."

Michael Huffington was an obscure Republican congressman from Santa Barbara who, being also an oil heir, had, indeed, decided to buy himself a seat in the Senate. He was in the process of spending $25 million.

On a per-person basis, that was not the most that had ever been spent in a state election. But in dollars it was the most. Look at the size this way: In presidential elections—among the very few to be funded by taxpayers—the federal government offered the parties $60 million each and forbade them from spending any more if they took the money. Major loopholes in that arrangement developed in 1996, but the point remains: the federal government had decided that the appropriate spending level for a national campaign was not much more than twice what Huffington was spending in one state.

Huffington was universally considered an empty vessel by those who watched him, a man who had nothing going for him but money. And yet he closed the gap in the polls with Democratic incumbent Dianne Feinstein. Not without reason were the national media and the political community generally transfixed by California.

One newspaper quoted Larry Berg, director of the Unruh Institute of Politics at the University of Southern California, as saying: "I always thought there was a limit to what money could do in politics. But I'm having to re-evaluate that now. Huffington is different from a Rockefeller or a Kennedy. He is a political nobody. But he's spending more than any of them ever did. If he can pull this off, I'm not sure there is a limit to what money can buy."

Huffington had bought himself a seat in the House of Representatives a couple of years earlier. He did this by spending an unheard-of $5 million against seven-term incumbent Robert Lagomarsino in Santa Barbara in the Republican primary in a Republican district. Then, in 1994, he outspent his opponents to win the Senate primary.

The belief that he would actually buy a Senate seat flowed from an assumption that general elections are like primaries. Maybe they aren't. The fundamental task of a candidate in a hotly contested general election is simply defined: win the Independent voters.

This book offers no final word on how primaries work, on what the fundamental task of a candidate is. But here's a theory: If we are talking about an electorate (in a primary) that is dominated by voters with strong opinions on the issues, opinions that basically reflect those of the mainstream of a party, the candidate who is in the best position to convince voters that he has those views has a certain advantage. Money can be useful toward that goal under certain circumstances. But where—as in a general election—the decisive voters are not motivated by their views on controversies, but by their judgments of the record and reputation of the incumbent, money in the hands of the challenger is likely to be less useful.

The anecdotal evidence that money proves most useful in primaries is abundant. In 1990, a millionaire named Clayton Williams re-invented himself as a politician and blew away all competition for the Republican nomination for governor of Texas, including that from professional politicians. He went into the general election against a non-incumbent Ann Richards with a big lead in the polls and a huge lead in money. A Huffington-like alarm spread through political circles about how the millionaires were taking over, how nobody else could afford to campaign in a state as big as Texas, with as many media markets. But the millionaire lost.

True, other millionaires have won statewide general elections; the U.S. Senate is full of them. But the conditions have to be right for their party. Most likely, in most cases, the experienced politicians they beat in the primaries—or scared out of running in the primaries—would have won in the generals, just as the millionaires did, if they had gotten that far. That, at least, is the logic of the keys in Senate races.

Back to California, 1994: Feinstein won, 47-45 percent. It was not easy, and the media generally attributed her success to a late flap that struck the Huffington campaign. Turned out he had been employing an illegal alien in a domestic position even as he had supported clamping down on immigration, saying that he wanted Americans to have better shots at jobs.

The immigration issue coincided with his fall in the polls. So, automatically, the political community decided the issue caused his decline. That's understandable. If you start from the assumption that campaign events are important causes of victory and defeat, then you look for campaign events to explain any given outcome. And, because campaigns are complex things, there's always something to point to.

But the alien explanation is highly dubious. Look at all the other "embarrassments" Huffington had to deal with. He was a carpetbagger, having only come to California recently; he had no accomplishments in office to point to; he was being opposed by respected Republicans, including the mayor of Los Angeles; he unmistakably had the image of guy who was simply trying to buy a Senate seat.

But the conventional wisdom doesn't cite any of these factors as reasons for his defeat, because these factors were all present when he was moving up in the polls.

Again, the polls. But what if the polls were taken before the decisive voters really focused?

An afterword about California: The California political community and the national political people who are fascinated by California politics learned nothing about the role of money from the comeuppance given to the monumentally funded candidate in 1994. In 1998, a candidate for governor, Democrat Al Checchi, spent more money in the primary than Huffington had spent in the general election. Checchi, too, was widely described in the media during the campaign not simply as trying to buy the election, but as succeeding. He, too, lost.

Lt. Gov. Gray Davis—whose personality and stump style were likened to his name more often than Ted Kennedy was said to be in the fight of his life—spent far less than either Checchi or another candidate and came from behind to win. (So, even in primaries, money—even in breathtaking amounts—is apparently not the be-all and end-all.)

Gray's victory did not happen because he went into the race with an advantage in name recognition. We know this, because, although he started the campaign ahead in the polls, he dropped into a very poor third after the television commercials began. He won because something happened after he had fallen behind, after whatever advantage he had in name recognition had been overcome. What happened was probably just that voters finally focused on the decision at hand, and, when they did, they saw no reason to go against the guy with the experience. (Contrast that with the New Jersey Democratic primary in 2000, in which a millionaire novice beat a former governor whom there was plenty of reason to vote against: he had raised taxes a lot immediately after promising not to.)

Typical of the journalism about the 1998 race was a major article a month before the primary in *The New Republic,* which is supposed to be a source to which political professionals and aficionados can turn for particularly sophisticated analysis of American politics. This article was premised on the fact that Gray Davis didn't have enough money to compete. It was a hand-wringer about what Checchi's success tells us about the state of American politics.

Peter Beinart wrote, "Gray Davis (will) spend around $7 million by primary day…. In California this year, that isn't enough."

The article was written at a time when "Polls show (Congresswoman Jane Harman) running a close second to Checchi, with Davis far back." The writer apparently couldn't imagine what could bring Davis to the top.

Conventional political analysis suggested to him that there wasn't anything. After the fact, of course, other analysts found things. Commentator and activist Arianna Huffington (former wife of the aforementioned Huffington) thought Checchi went too "negative" in his ads at the advice of national political consultants; that view was widely heard. Commentator Dan Walters, in *The Sacramento Bee*, listed many Checchi campaign mistakes as the explanation. (Checchi put forth an unfocused pitch, tried to be all things to all people—rather than a liberal or conservative—offered a spending plan that didn't add up, refused to respond to criticism of it, and more.)

If, however, exactly the same events had taken place, and Checchi had won, none of the commentators would have been the least bit surprised. The same people who ended up criticizing his campaign would have embraced it as brilliant. They would have said, see, going negative works, as they always do after every campaign in which a negative campaigner wins. And, see, the money with which to go negative is crucial.

Most likely, though, Checchi would have lost even if he had gone the route of the Monday-morning quarterbacks. He was getting the best advice money could buy, after all. That fact has to figure into the analyses someplace. The pundits want us to believe they know better than the people Checchi paid, but they can offer us no reason to believe that, except that Checchi lost, which is only a reason if you buy into the campaigns-count theology in the first place. At any rate, the possibility that he ran the best possible race is counter-intuitive for most people, because he lost his lead in the polls.

Again, the polls.

But if mere campaign events (bad ads, muddy answers, whatever) were enough to offset the supposedly historic, monumental advantage that Checchi started with, maybe that monumental advantage wasn't so monumental, after all.

Back to 1994.

Virginia

A story from Knight-Ridder news service, in *The Philadelphia Inquirer* of Jan. 28, 1994, was headlined:

"North Makes It Official;

He's Running for Senate from Va.

He Was Once Convicted in the Iran-Contra Case

Incumbent Charles S. Robb Is Seen as Vulnerable"

The piece's first paragraph said, "North (told) 500 supporters at a hotel rally that he is a 'conservative outsider' who will 'strike a blow to give government back to the people.'"

The liberal *Nation* magazine devoted a cover story as late as Oct. 24 to its nightmare: "Fear and Loathing in North Country," read the headline. "Why Ollie Will Win."

Such predictions were not uncommon. After all, during the Iran-Contra congressional hearings in 1987, North had become so popular in the polls that he was widely being called "an American hero." He is a gifted communicator; he has a certain touch. And, because he had stood up to Congress, he was sort of the anti-Senator.

We are, after all, talking about an anti-politician era. This was the year when term-limits fever reached its peak, when politicians thought they could do nothing better for their candidacies than to promise not to stay in Washington very long. In a decade when legislators by the droves were doing everything possible to convince voters that they were of the people, not of the institution, North's political positioning seemed perfect.

He won at the state party convention over a strong candidate (a former director of the federal budget) in part because he had the support of the Religious Right, which was seen as a mighty force nationally, and all the mightier in Virginia among Republicans.

Early polls did not show North beating Robb. Nevertheless, he always made the list of Senate races the Republicans would win if they won the Senate.

Today Oliver North's role in electoral history is that, running as a right-wing Republican in one of the most conservative states in the nation in the most Republican year in memory, against a Democratic incumbent who was badly damaged by a scandal badly handled, and running with a 4-1 advantage in money, he managed to lose anyway.

If, in other words, there is such a thing as a strong candidate or a weak candidate, Oliver North was an extraordinarily weak candidate.

In 1994, the media got caught up in all the glitzy stuff surrounding North, Huffington and Romney—money, looks, fame, charisma—that the conventional wisdom is so fascinated with, and that hardly matters, at least in determining the outcomes of general elections.

Meanwhile, nobody saw the tidal wave coming. But tidal waves are not invisible.

Flaw in Senate Keys Emerges

What about Lichtman? Well, if the tone of the foregoing part of this chapter is smug and superior in its approach to media pundits, that cannot be justified with a look at Lichtman's record in 1994. The justification will have to rest on other years.

In 1994, Lichtman missed 8 out of 35 races, a record that looks somewhat worse when you figure that a lot of the 35 weren't in any degree of doubt from day one. (Actually, Lichtman's 77-percent success rate might compare favorably with just about anybody else's. But finding people who made flat predictions in all 35 is not easy. Let's just say 77 percent—counting obvious calls—is not what Lichtman is going for.)

The keys had no difficulty with the Kennedy election. An incumbent needs four keys to get a prediction of victory. Kennedy started with five: he was the incumbent, a national figure, the consensus choice of the party for nomination, and a 65-percent winner his last time out, and his opponent was not a national figure or governor or congressman.

However, the keys were wrong on both California and Virginia, predicting problems for both Democratic incumbents. Feinstein, besides being outspent, was not a national figure, did not have a big win behind her, was opposed by a congressman, and was running in a midterm while her party held the presidency. Five keys down. Normally that would have been enough. But apparently Huffington—far from being the exceptionally strong candidate the media saw at one stage—was just so exceptionally offensive to people that having the keys on his side and an historically great year for Republicans and a monumental amount of money was not enough.

In Virginia, North also had five keys going for him. He was a national figure who survived a tough fight for the nomination (getting 55 percent of the vote at the state convention), which got him a key; he had more money than Robb, who was not a national figure; and North benefited from being the GOP candidate in a midterm election when the Democrats had the White House.

If only he wasn't such a joke.

A couple of mistakes like this are normal for the keys in a Senate season. Peculiar local situations arise.

What was exceptional about 1994 for the keys was not that Republicans managed to find a way to lose a couple of races they could have won. What was exceptional was that Lichtman predicted a whole bunch of Democratic victories where Republican victories occurred. The keys did not see Democratic Sen. Harris Wofford losing his Pennsylvania seat to Rep. Rick Santorum. They did not see veteran Sen. Jim Sasser losing to Republican novice Bill Frist in Tennessee, or Republican Fred Thompson taking the open seat there that Al Gore had vacated to become vice president. The keys also failed to see Republican victories coming in open seats in Oklahoma, Missouri and Minnesota.

In most years, the mistakes the keys make in Senate races have no partisan pattern; the keys are as likely to mistakenly predict a Democrat over a Republican as a Republican over a Democrat. The fact that there was a partisan pattern in 1994 makes clear just how and why the keys failed: they, too, failed to pick up the national Republican tidal wave.

Though Lichtman is a liberal Democrat (running in 2006 for the U.S. Senate in Maryland), that is clearly not the explanation. Nothing in his keys favors Democrats. Nothing in his predictive record—including on the presidential side—before 1994 indicated a tendency toward excessive partisan optimism. And, obviously, he does not help his own reputation if his predictions are partisan and wrong.

The problem in 1994 was that the Senate keys are not equipped to handle an election in which a particular party has a special surge. No midterm election like 1994 had occurred in the period Lichtman had tested his keys against: 1970-1984. Maybe American politics somehow changed in the 1990s.

The Senate keys were developed by studying more races than the presidential keys, simply because there are more Senate races. But they covered only one brief period of history. Lichtman has always had less interest and less confidence in them than in the presidential keys.

Still, he is the first to say the presidential keys will fail someday, too. That is one prediction you can rely upon for sure.

Lichtman tried to tweak his Senate system after 1994—to find a way to take the possibility of a national party surge into account—but he found that when he applied any new keys to past elections, they caused at least as many new errors in predictions as new successes.

Let's just settle for saying the Lichtman system is not perfect. Though 1994 was the first Senate election (out of 5) in which Lichtman did not reach his 90-percent goal, it was not the last. (In 2000, the keys underestimated Democratic strength.) In general, the keys were not as effective after 1994 as they were before. So it's entirely possible that the keys Lichtman arrived at by looking at races between 1970 and 1984 for the best predictors are not the ones he would arrive at if he looked at, say, 1980 through 2002. For one thing, the scarcity of primaries these days—as party leaders try to head off such contests as threats to party unity and funds, and as candidates without money get scared off by millionaires—may render the keys relating to primaries less useful.

At any rate, over the last 10 elections, the system has had an overall success percentage in the high 80s, with most individual years being around 90.

CHAPTER

9

2000 – Even Gore's Ineptitude Couldn't Thwart the Keys

Let's apply the keys to the 2000 presidential election. (To review: six or more "false" answers, and the challenging party wins the popular vote):

Key 1 (Party Mandate): *After the midterm elections (that is, 1998), the incumbent (i.e., presidential) party holds more seats in the U.S. House of Representatives than it did after the previous midterm elections.*

The Democrats gained House seats not only in 1996, but—breaking a long historical pattern for parties with the presidency—in 1998. This key gets a "**true**" answer, going for Gore.

Key 2 (Contest): *There is no serious contest for the incumbent-party nomination.*

If Sen. Bill Bradley had been able to stay in the race until the Democratic convention and had gotten more than a third of the votes there on the first ballot, he would have caused Gore problems in the general election. As things turned out, there was no serious contest. **True.**

Key 3 (Incumbency): *The incumbent-party candidate is the sitting president.*

If Clinton had been removed from office via the impeachment process, Gore would have gotten this key. But, **false.**

Key 4 (Third Party): *There is no significant third-party or Independent campaign.*

As noted earlier, 5 percent is Lichtman's rule of thumb for the support a third candidate must have to turn the key against the incumbents. Reform Party candidate Pat Buchanan ran generally at only about 2 percent in the polls. More interesting was the Ralph Nader/Green Party effort. Nader was showing at 6 or 7 percent in national polls in early July. But a third-party candidate's vote usually turns out to be about half of what it looks like at its peak. A good guess was that Nader would be hurt by the reluctance of liberal voters to elect a Republican president. So Lichtman turned the key in the direction of **true**—there was no major third-party candidate. In the end, Nader ran way below half of what he was polling in the summer (even if his tally exceeded the gap between the major-party candidates in microscopically close Florida).

Key 5 (Short-term economy): *The economy is not in recession during the election campaign.* **True.**

Key 6 (Long-term economy): *Real per-capita economic growth during the current presidential term equals or exceeds mean growth during the previous two terms.*

Clinton's first term saw more economic growth than George Bush's presidency, and Clinton's second term was even better than his first. **True.**

Key 7 (Policy change): *The incumbent administration effects major changes in national policy.*

Nothing happened comparable to Reagan's first term, Lyndon Johnson's term or Franklin Roosevelt's first term. That's the standard. **False.**

Key 8 (Social unrest): *There is no sustained social unrest during the term.* **True.**

Key 9 (Scandal): *The incumbent administration is untainted by major scandal.*

Impeachment is pretty major, even if it's partisan. This key requires that the presence of scandal is accepted across a bipartisan spectrum. Though the parties split on impeachment, pretty much everybody perceived a scandal. The existence of other, smaller scandals besides the Monica Lewinsky case sealed the deal. **False.**

Key 10 (Foreign/military failure): *The incumbent administration suffers no major failure in foreign or military affairs.* **True.**

Key 11 (Foreign/military success): *The incumbent administration achieves a major success in foreign or military affairs.*

The Kosovo air war was successful in the sense that the other side gave up. But that was not enough to turn a key, any more than the Clinton administration's success in bringing (a difficult) peace to Bosnia did in his first term. These issues did not have the direct connection to American interests that are necessary. They did not greatly improve the American international situation. **False.**

Key 12 (Incumbent charisma): *The incumbent-party candidate is charismatic or a national hero.*

Gore? **False.**

Key 13 (Challenger charisma): *The challenging-party candidate is not charismatic or a national hero.*

Note the question in keys 12 and 13 is not which candidate is more charismatic, but does either have a special Reagan-like quality. George W. Bush is not in that league. **True.**

Five falses. Gore wins.

That is, he wins the popular vote. Gore won by a half million votes, not such a tiny amount by historic standards. It's as much as Richard Nixon won by in 1968, and several times more than John Kennedy's margin in 1960.

Obviously, the fact that George W. Bush is president is an unpleasant one from the point of view of anybody who predicted only a Gore victory. After I claimed victory for the keys in 2000 I was accused by one colleague of saying the operation was a success, even though the patient died.

But come on! The Electoral College is such a strangely designed mechanism that one has difficulty imagining a system that could predict how it would go with any more accuracy than a system which focuses on the popular vote and hopes for the best in the Electoral College. If Lichtman had managed to come up with one set of keys that gets all post-Civil War races correct as to the popular vote, and another that gets them all correct on the Electoral College, what might the difference be? Most likely, it would be analytically unconvincing. That is, the splits between the Electoral College and the popular vote may be completely random, reflecting no logic. And if somebody could give a system that has no logic but has worked three times (that is, whenever the Electoral College has split off from the popular vote) would you really have any interest in it?

Once in a century, a quirky mechanism has intervened between the votes of the people and the outcome of the election. To try to figure out when and why that might happen would be an entirely different undertaking from Lichtman's.

———

The success of the keys in calling Gore's popular-vote victory was an almost singular success. It separated Lichtman not only from conventional journalistic wisdom but from his academic colleagues.

The keys pointed to a Gore victory over George W. Bush starting in mid-1999, when Bush was soaring in the polls and the conventional journalistic wisdom was going along mindlessly. The candidates had their ups and downs after that. The keys continued to point to Gore through the dark days of October 2000, when Bush regained and held a lead in the polls. That lead got up to double digits in the CNN/*USA Today*/Gallup Poll.

When, on the day before the election, one major poll (Zogby) showed a one-point lead for Gore, it was the first poll in weeks to show a Gore lead and the only one on that day.

Political junkies will remember that in the last days of the campaign the pundits had it exactly backwards. They were giving the popular vote to Bush and wondering if maybe Gore could win the Electoral College. It was a wonderfully classic case of mass-media mass confusion.

Reuters news service, on Nov. 1: "Analysts are increasingly discussing the possibility of Bush winning the popular vote by piling up huge margins in the South and losing in the Electoral College." The *Los Angeles Times,* on Oct. 26: Analysts "are weighing scenarios under which" George W. Bush could win the popular vote but lose the Electoral College. *The New*

York Times, on Nov. 6, the day before the election: "To be sure, the race is so tight that some say it is possible for one candidate—most likely Mr. Gore—to lose the popular vote and win in the Electoral College."

A political insiders' publication called *The Bulletin's Frontrunner* ran a piece on Nov. 1 labeled "Bush Leading All National Tracking Polls Again," a point its headlines made repeatedly that week. In the piece it said, "(A)n American Research Group analysis of the Electoral College shows 'the national popular-vote polls do not reflect the state-by-state dynamics of the electoral vote. ARG's analysis of the electoral-vote count, including results of surveys being conducted in Florida, Michigan, New Hampshire, Pennsylvania, and Tennessee, shows Al Gore with 274 electoral votes, enough to win the presidency.'"

In the aftermath of the campaign, one often hears from the media that the surprising thing is that Gore didn't win easily, given the nation's peace and prosperity. But the notion that 2000 should be a Gore year didn't develop in the media generally until after the Democratic convention, when—with one speech—Gore wiped out a big, yearlong (and totally meaningless) Bush lead in the polls.

Before that, the political media were busy explaining all the Democrats' problems: "Clinton fatigue;" Gore's own ethical lapses; Gore's woodenness; Bush's likable personality; Bush's incredible amounts of campaign money; Republican determination, after years out of the presidency; the public's instinctive taste for change; the soaring price of gasoline; you name it.

In early May, conventional, high-profile political analyst Stuart Rothenberg, the kind of guy to whom journalists turn for insights, said, "All the indications are that Bush has an edge in the race and that Gore is the underdog, which is unbelievable given the strong economy and what Bush went through in the primaries."

Whatever emphasis the pundits may have put on the importance of the economy after the election, they had no difficulty explaining before the conventions—with Bush ahead—why it didn't matter much. A poll-driven George Will wrote in August 2000, about the "perverse... political consequences of prosperity.... Americans are feeling so flush, the economy has lost saliency as a political issue."

In the aftermath of a paper-thin election, a pre-election insistence that Gore had some major problems does not look absurd. However, the prolonged absence in the media of references to Bush's political problems—an absence that is difficult to document, because of the nature of absences—does look absurd.

More important, a paper-thin election was not necessarily what people were expecting. When a version of this book was posted on the Internet in the spring of 2000, my friends in journalism responded to its prediction as follows:

"Omigod! You're picking Gore!"

From one particularly experienced and astute observer (at the end of July), "The keys are pretty clear and Gore should win. That said, it sure doesn't feel like it as we sit here today."

And, from another political journalist: "Here's my problem, or (at least) one of them: I simply cannot sit here at my desk in front of my computer on June 28, 2000 A.D. and believe that the American people are going to elect Albert Gore Jr. I cannot. Americans don't like him. They have never liked him. And as someone else said, the American people won't vote for someone they don't like unless they're absolutely forced to."

Keep in mind that these were my friends, people who were trying to be gentle (and who did, in fact, say they saw some merit in the book).

What about the political scientists with predictive schemes? They were definitely in a different frame of mind. As noted in Chapter 3, a half-dozen political scientists—and teams of political scientists—who have their own predictive schemes were agreeing with historian Lichtman that Gore would win.

Unfortunately for them, though, they were saying Gore would win comfortably, even easily. One of them had Gore getting 59 percent of the two-party popular vote, a landslide beyond anything any nonincumbent has ever won.

Unlike the political scientists, Lichtman does not predict what the margin of victory will be. But he said his prediction was a very close call, in the sense that the factors he looks at were pointing in both directions. The political scientists made the mistake of focusing almost entirely on the economy and on various kinds of polls about public satisfaction with the president, the direction of the country and the nature of the economy. Those are not the only things that matter.

The 2000 race made five presidential-election predictions in a row that the Lichtman scheme has gotten right since he invented it, if you count the disputed 1992. And if anybody says most of those calls were obvious, I will scream. They absolutely were not.

Having said all that, the 2000 election did give me fits. It not only left me worried in October about the accuracy of the prediction. It offered exceptions to some rules I proposed in the e-version of this book that was posted that year. I had insisted, for example, that presidential elections are not best seen as 50 different elections, as some see them, but as one great big election. That is, a national tide generally sweeps the country, if sometimes at the last minute. That's why, I said, the Electoral College is generally more lopsided than the popular vote.

Well, this time there was a late Gore tide. But its effect was to make the election so close in some places that local factors ended up mattering a lot.

(Let the record show that the one-great-big-election theory, repeated in this version, is a Gottlieb extrapolation, not part of the original Lichtman scripture.)

More important, Gore campaigned so incredibly badly as to provide a difficult test for the theory that campaigns don't matter much. He failed to recognize what he should have known as a reader of the keys (which he is): his great card was President Bill Clinton's record.

One would have expected Gore to remind the country again and again how incredibly far it had come in eight years, not only as to the economy, but on welfare rates, crime rates, the deficit, and more. He should have evoked again and again how dispirited the country was in 1992, how confused (to the point of considering Ross Perot), how angry (to the point of being fixated on term limits).

Instead, Gore was spooked by the Clinton scandals into largely ignoring the past. He allowed Bush to make 2000 the starting point for every policy debate, rather than 1992. Asked about education, as the supposed No. 1 public concern in 2000, Gore should have, for example, pointed out how many other issues were seen as more pressing in 1992. Education came to the front only because the economy, the deficit, crime and drugs receded, as foreign policy had receded before them.

The logic of the notion that campaigns don't count is not that the candidates needn't bother campaigning, that everything is pre-determined. The logic is that the candidates' predictably energetic efforts generally will cancel each other out. Both campaigns will be cleverly conceived by the best counselors money can buy, but somewhat flawed in execution. Both will experience some embarrassments and setbacks. It's a long year. In the end, though, underlying circumstances will determine the outcome of the election.

In the long run, the system will probably be wrong about 10 percent of the time. Gore almost made 2000 the first time. He was bad enough to mess up the Electoral College.

But even *he* wasn't quite bad enough to mess up the Lichtman keys.

CHAPTER

10

2004 – Never Close

I sent this book out to traditional publishers in the fall of 2003, the idea being to get it published in 2004. I had always proceeded on the premise that publishers would see the book as marketable only in connection with a presidential election. That turned out to be pretty much true. However, more than one publisher suggested that my timing was a little off, anyway, because they already had their plans for 2004.

Rather than wait until 2008, I decided to use print-on-demand (or self-) publishing. One reason was that I wanted 2004 to be fresh in readers' minds, so they wouldn't have to rely on my documentation of what the media were saying during the campaign and after.

What the journalistic predictors were doing in 2004 was essentially nothing. Oh, sure, a few partisans said the guy they favored was going to win, because the American people are smart, and all that.

For the most part, though, even partisans avoided that sort of thing. By normal standards, the race was just *way* too close to call from mid-spring through fall. For many months leading up to the Democratic convention, the polls were consistently saying that neither side had a statistically significant edge. Then even that convention failed to move the numbers. This locked in the notion that 2004 was a year of immutable and extraordinary polarization, with a tiny percentage of people holding the balance of power.

The outcome was almost universally seen as depending upon future events. In the June 29 *Washington Post,* columnist E.J. Dionne surveyed what other pundits were saying, and reluctantly agreed: "Some pundit's handbook no doubt warns prognosticators to attach caveats to all predictions. So, yes, how this election turns out will depend a great deal on how the situation in Iraq looks to voters on Election Day, and how many middle-class and blue-collar voters feel the economic recovery in their own lives by then."

Eventually, however, the Republican convention did open a significant gap in favor of George W. Bush; so much for the immutability theory.

As Bush's lead held for a few weeks, some people started saying that John Kerry had blown it with a convention that was all about his military record and had no substance, or that he had responded too slowly and lamely to the "Swift Boat" television ads, which denounced his military record. Some people called the race over at this point. But even that turned out not to be true, as Bush's poll lead evaporated in the wake of the debates. Once again, everybody was back to "too close to call."

And then there was me. I hereby justify quoting myself immodestly: I have learned never to believe anybody who claims to have predicted something but can't document the prediction, certainly not somebody who writes for a living. Willingness to put predictions in writing repeatedly— and risk embarrassment—is a measure of seriousness, of whether one is talking through one's hat.

Anyway, it's not even me doing the predicting. I was just channeling Lichtman, just plugging in the data. It's not a great accomplishment; it's just recognition of another's success.

On January 7, 2004, well before anybody knew who the Democratic nominee might be, I wrote a column for the *Dayton Daily News* labeled "Bush Has Won 2004 Election."

"We may not know for sure," it began, "who actually won the election of 2000, but we know who won in 2004.

"George W. Bush did. He won gradually, when he brought down the Taliban government of Afghanistan and the regime in Iraq and captured Saddam Hussein; when the American economy turned up in late 2003; when his party prospered under his leadership, as measured by its gains in the 2002 election, and when his first term turned out not to be marred by major, historic scandal or major social unrest.

"Theoretically, this prediction could still be overturned by events, but those events—plural—would have to be really big ones, the like of which never happen in an election year.

"The system that underlies this prediction focuses on the prevailing conditions in the election year. Nobody can say for sure that scandal and social unrest won't occur. But one or the other alone wouldn't be enough.

"Nor would bad news in Iraq or elsewhere in foreign policy....

"If the bad news were bad enough to, say, weaken Bush so much as to encourage a third-party movement or to undermine Republican unity, that could matter. But that's seriously unlikely....

"It doesn't matter whom the Democrats nominate. Their decision might affect the margin of defeat, but not the fact of defeat....

"Forget Bush's money, and Karl Rove's political talent and who the Democrats pick for vice president and all that other stuff that gets massaged endlessly in an election year by the alleged experts in the media. The big-picture realities of 2004 are made for an incumbent party."

This prediction of a Bush victory didn't surprise many. He was, after all, up in the polls. And the Democrats had a bunch of non-entities running around New Hampshire and Iowa, none of them looking presidential. There was a buzz around Howard Dean and his then-unprecedented ability to raise money over the Internet, but many professionals thought his nomination would be a disaster. John Kerry was back in the pack.

When, however, Kerry suddenly emerged in Iowa and New Hampshire, he developed a glow around him that put him ahead of Bush in the polls. All of a sudden, the Democrats were very excited indeed. They thought they had picked the most likely winner, a war hero of presidential demeanor, unlike Dean. The money was pouring in for them. Everything was looking good.

So, trying to be as helpful as I could, I reiterated on March 5:

"Bush Still Wins Prediction: The factors he had going for him when his polls were good are still there." I made the point still more times as the year proceeded, never wavering, if I do say so myself.

This is not to say that I was certain at every moment of every day. I was not. I have always believed the keys will be wrong someday. During the summer, despite deadlocked polls, it occurred to me that Kerry might be seen as having an edge, because he seemed more likely than Bush to benefit from his convention. After all, he was less known going in, and there was more room for movement.

The last days of the campaign were a difficult time to stick with Lichtman with certitude. The general consensus in Ohio was that Kerry was coming on strong there, that he had out-organized Bush, that, in a campaign that had been close almost all along, things had fallen his way at the end, including the debates. His "Swift Boat" critics had been discredited and the issue had seemingly disappeared. Beloved octogenarian John Glenn was showing up at almost every Kerry rally, adding a special touch. And those rallies had a good feel. (Bush had bigger rallies, but they were in heavily Republican areas. Kerry was going to the battlegrounds.)

I was trying in that period to be in touch with the politicos. The Republicans—who hadn't been happy all year—were increasingly pessimistic, apparently not liking their own polls. The Democrats were increasingly optimistic.

If you thought Kerry was going to win Ohio, you pretty much thought he was going to win the election, so pivotal was that state.

On Election Day, itself, anybody working at a newspaper knew that the exit polls were showing Kerry, both nationally and statewide.

Talk about mixed emotions: As a voter, I was very strongly for Kerry. As a guy with a book to publish and sell, not so much.

I felt that if Kerry won I would be known forever in political circles in and near Dayton as the know-it-all pundit who was wrong on the big one. I would be offering up a classic case of the kind of pundit-corps incompetence I write about. I did not relish the irony.

All year, everywhere I went, it seemed that what everybody wanted to talk about was my prediction about the election. Democrats generally were as optimistic about Kerry as they had been pessimistic about Gore. They thought that a year when the Democrats have money, enthusiasm and a decorated war vet is a Democratic year, at least when the economy has been generally weak for several years, the president is not particularly popular, and a war that was essentially declared won months earlier is starting to drag on.

What I said worried some people, convinced nobody, near as I know.

I harped on the subject in print not, as I say, out of certainty, but out of the feeling that familiarity with the Lichtman record was best thing

I brought to the table after a lifetime of political observation and two decades as a professional commentator.

That call was not close.

I felt, in fact, that this stuff was more useful for people trying to understand the forces at work in an American presidential election than the best work of my betters in my field.

As for the 2004 predictions, the deal was this: by the beginning of the year, it was difficult to find six keys that might turn against Bush.

His party had gained House seats in the 2002 election, suggesting that party label would be no problem for Bush, and locking in one key. He would be the incumbent (a second key) and would be renominated easily (a third). He was not facing any third-party threat (fourth key); even in January, to count Ralph Nader against Bush would have been absurd.

The economy was going upwards, not downwards, and no recession was likely during the campaign. So, while the Democrats would pick up one key for the long-term economy, the Republicans would get their fifth for the short-term economy.

There was no social unrest to speak of. And the Democrats were not going to put up a charismatic candidate. (John Kerry's medals, even taken at face value, don't come close to making him a national hero, a la Dwight Eisenhower.)

So those seven keys were essentially out of play. The Democrats needed all the rest to fall their way.

Besides the long-term economy, they had Bush's lack of charisma. From there, it was tough.

Scandal? Some Democrats were scandalized by the way the country entered the war in Iraq, with the president saying all manner of things that turned out not to be true. But that's not the sort of scandal that turns a key. Something unexpected and big needs to happen. People don't expect politicians to speak the truth. They only expect presidents and their top cronies to stay out of trouble with the law.

There were corporate scandals—especially Enron—that the Democrats would have liked the public to see as Republican scandals. But that, too, is not how the keys work. The trouble has to be closer to home.

So far we have not mentioned three keys: the two on foreign policy (success and failure) and one on policy change. They were the most interesting in 2004. But even if they all went for Kerry, Bush would have won the prediction.

In the end, one went for Bush. Let's start with one that didn't: foreign-policy failure.

The very, very, very oft-heard "prediction" that the election outcome would depend upon how the war went reflected unfamiliarity with the keys. In truth, Bush lost the foreign-policy-failure key on 9-11. And there's only one such key. Bad news in Iraq couldn't turn another, unless it was so bad as to, say, foster a challenge to his renomination or foster a third party.

Counting 9-11 against him seems counterintuitive to some people. They see it as a political boon to Bush, because people rallied around him, and his popularity ratings soared, and because, after all, the attack wasn't his fault. But Pearl Harbor also turned a key against Franklin D. Roosevelt. The logic—again, derived from historical patterns—is this: people do not like to see bad news—the country hurt in some way—that goes uncorrected.

So, in making a prediction, first you turn that bad-news key against the incumbent. Then you look to see what, in the new political situation, he does about other keys.

Bush turned a key in his favor by winning a war in Afghanistan, eliminating the America-threatening Taliban, with few American losses, when Americans were feeling vulnerable. That victory might not look like much now, but it was a robust, successful response to a crisis.

As for the policy-change key—wherein a president gets a key for being a successful agent of historic change—it was a close call. Lichtman did not give it to Bush, though Bush had set out to be an activist president even before 9-11. He had pushed an agenda of tax cuts, a major new role for the feds in public education, support for faith-based social programs, and a new kind of foreign policy, entailing a form of unilateralism. After 9-11, Bush far more dramatically redesigned American foreign policy to be all about the war on terror. And the government was reorganized to create the Department of Homeland Security.

But much of the response to 9-11 seemed forced upon the government, and much was bipartisan, rather than originating with Bush. The big exception was, of course, the Iraq war. But starting a war—even on a new kind of rationale (pre-emption)—has never been seen as policy change of the kind that turns keys.

Moreover, the run-up to the war and the war itself had the effect of stalling Bush domestic initiatives in Congress, rather than facilitating them. So the mark he himself made wasn't historic.

It's ironic: if Bush had governed entirely with the keys in mind, he would have proceeded as he did, both in the domestic and international realms, always opting for action—big action—and change.

That didn't directly turn any keys for him except for the one about foreign-policy success, which he didn't need and which any president would likely have won, because the attack on Afghanistan seemed so obviously called for.

And yet, establishing himself as a strong, forceful leader might have helped the party make the congressional gains in 2002 that turned a key. It might have helped keep the party united, and might have prevented, say, Sen. John McCain from seeing an opening for a third party in the election. And Bush's insistence on the most expensive tax cuts he could get—part of the overall strategy of activism—might have assured that the economy would turn up before the election.

At any rate, despite all the post-election analysis, the outcome of the election wasn't about the Democrats not "getting" values. It wasn't about the evangelicals being energized by the gay marriage issue on many ballots, or about Kerry being too liberal or wishy-washy or a patrician, or the Republicans doing better on turnout. It wasn't about television ads.

Things simply went about as well on George W. Bush's watch as swing voters expect them to go.

With the keys breaking 9-4 for him, the question the pundits should have agonized over after the election was not why an incumbent won—and not what's wrong with the Democrats—but why the Democrats were able to make it so close.

CHAPTER

11

Progress: Bush (or Rove) Gets the Point

The reason George H.W. Bush lost the presidency in 1992 has changed, albeit subtly.

Originally, the reason was "the economy." No number of citations will convince the appropriately skeptical reader that that explanation was offered more than any other. (Others were offered, too.) But just think about all the times you have heard "It's the economy, stupid," offered as the explanation.

Immediately after the election, reporters Tom Diemer and John Funk, of the Cleveland *Plain Dealer*, surveyed Ohio's political leaders for their explanation for Clinton's victory in that swing state. The Democratic Party's state chairman, Jim Ruvulo, offered this interpretation: "The economy, the economy, the economy."

The Republican chairman also said it was the economy, in a sense.

"The people who couldn't bring themselves to go vote for Clinton and yet were upset with the economic situation found it very comfortable to go to Perot," said Robert Bennett.

The reporters added: "The economy indeed was the dominant theme for Ohio voters this fall, according to exit poll findings." In those polls, nearly twice as many voters singled the economy out as an important issue than mentioned any other.

By 2002, though, the reason Bush lost was not so much "the economy" as the way Bush dealt with the economy as president and as candidate. The distinction is important, because the condition of "the economy" can be a matter of mere luck. And because traditional political analysts sometimes accord "the economy"—that is, the numbers, pure and simple—almost holy status as a shaper of elections. If the pundits are talking not only about the numbers, but also about what the president does, they are talking about policy—or perhaps just about media manipulation, depending on what the president is actually doing.

As the political pundits pondered the 2004 election, starting in 2002, they nearly all found fascinating similarities between the two Presidents Bush. Most specifically, both had presided over military victories and troublesome economies. Both experienced very high poll ratings that seemed to reflect public satisfaction with their records in national security issues. But then the first President Bush lost an election that focused on the economy. Would the second?

Note the treatment of the role of the economy in 1992 in three pieces done by reporters in April 2003:

From *The Mercury News* of San Jose: "The president has continued to focus on the troubled economy while articulating a well-defined and consistent plan to revive it. Whether or not his tax cuts revive the economy, his opponents will have a hard time portraying him as unconcerned or criticizing him for failing to offer a coherent plan, as they did with his father."

From *USA Today:* "White House advisers are increasingly concerned that Bush needs to convince Americans he is trying to reverse gloomy economic trends, caused in part by corporations delaying hiring and expansion plans until after the war. The advisers want him to avoid his father's fate."

The Detroit News quoted economist Bruce Bartlett of the National Center for Policy Analysis: "In 1992, the economy was doing fairly well, but people didn't perceive it that way. The belief among many Republicans is that the first George Bush lost not because he had a bad economy but because it was perceived that he didn't care. So Republicans think as long as they can go to the voters and say, 'We gave it our best shot,' voters will be kinder to them than the first President Bush."

The change in conventional wisdom about 1992—from "The economy was bad" to "Bush was too passive about the bad economy"—might, at first glance, be seen as regression from concern with objective reality (the numbers) to a concern with perceptions. But the new Bush people weren't settling for mere media events to demonstrate concern about the economy (though media events they certainly did stage). The president really was pushing for economic policy change, via his tax cuts.

Why did the conventional interpretation of 1992 change? One reason might be that the White House, whom the journalists are obliged to consult, offered off-the-record input that led reporters to think in terms of presidential activism and passivity, not simply the raw economic numbers.

Look at the Bush administration in the big picture. Here was a president who was a moderate governor of Texas, who, in fact, had high-profile support in the 2000 election from high-profile Texas Democrats. He ran a moderate campaign for president. He was the son of a moderate, establishment president. And he won the presidency with no mandate whatsoever for Republican policies. Yet, from the beginning, he ran an activist conservative administration, surprising both conservatives and liberals.

He pushed for tax cuts in 2001 that were far bigger than he had talked about during the campaign. He pushed for more in 2003, in fact so much as to surprise his own advisers. (*The New York Times* reported on Jan. 2, 2003 that "Mr. Bush is expected to propose a package of tax cuts worth as much as $300 billion over 10 years." The figure turned out, that week, to be over $700 billion.) Bush proposed historic changes in Social Security, in a conservative direction. He proposed new federal support for faith-based community groups dealing with social problems. Dismissing treaties, including the anti-ballistic missile treaty with the Russians, and proposed treaties, he set out on a unilateralist course in foreign policy that would have appalled the likes of his father.

In fact, the best way to understand the presidency was through this guideline: just about every time he faced a choice between action and inaction, he chose action. The most famous example was the Iraq war. Another was the Department of Homeland Security. Originally, he opposed the idea, preferring to have a White House official oversee that policy area, rather than a cabinet office (perhaps because a White House official can act in greater secrecy, a legitimate concern on security matters). But when some Democrats pushed the idea of a reorganization of the government and creation of a new cabinet department, he flip-flopped so aggressively that the whole idea became associated with him.

Senior and sober commentator David Broder called Bush's proposals as a whole a "radical" redirection of government policies.

Why? Where did this activism, this conservatism come from?

Bill Clinton was pretty much the same way, arguably more so. He got elected with no mandate, indeed with far less than half the popular vote. But he pushed ahead hard on an agenda that included a spending program to stimulate the economy (which Congress rejected), a tax increase, universal health care, welfare reform (which definitely was in his plans, even if not as soon as his conservative critics would have liked) and enactment of a wide range of Democratic initiatives that had been stalled in the first Bush presidency: motor voter, the Brady bill on gun control, family leave. And there was gay rights.

Moreover, he kept pressing even when he ran into bad polls and other political problems, on both taxes and health care, as well as on the North American Free Trade Agreement (NAFTA).

To some people, especially young people, to point out that particular presidents have had big agendas that they tried to get enacted may seem pointless. Isn't that what presidents try to do: enact their agendas? In fact, though, there have been both active and passive presidents. Dwight Eisenhower, John Kennedy and Richard Nixon, not to mention again George H.W. Bush, have been among the many who proceeded much more cautiously and slowly, or who never made any great effort to shake things up.

One might have expected both Clinton and the second Bush to be something less than full-blown activists, because the times in which they came to power did not seem propitious for the enactment of a major, sweeping program. They weren't in the position of Franklin D. Roosevelt, with a mandate to do something—just about anything—about the Great Depression. They weren't, like Lyndon Johnson, caught up in an historic national movement for change (civil rights). They weren't winners of landslide elections, the benefactors of huge congressional majorities for their parties. They didn't, like Ronald Reagan, campaign as advocates for a dramatically new approach to the issues, a dramatic deviation from the political center.

Typically, in the absence of such special factors, new presidents have been far more cautious.

Clinton and Bush were the first two presidents after the Lichtman keys became known to political animals. And the keys say to a politician (whether an officeholder, like Clinton, or confidant, like Karl Rove) that if one wants to be re-elected one should (1) get lucky (2) stay clean, (3) make major gains for the country in foreign policy or at least avoid setbacks, and (4) be an effective agent of change.

Being an agent of change didn't do it for Lyndon Johnson (or his party), in a time of unsuccessful war and social unrest. But it worked wonders for Ronald Reagan and Franklin Roosevelt, making them not only successful re-election candidates but historic figures.

And the most recent modern presidents who failed in re-election bids were most dramatically not effective agents of change: Gerald Ford, Jimmy Carter and George H.W. Bush.

Richard Nixon, as noted, doesn't rank with Roosevelt and Reagan as a change agent, but he did get a more solid grip on his office than those other three, did go to China, and did change American policy in Vietnam from a build-up to a build-down. And he only beat George McGovern.

If you look at the historical patterns that Lichtman gets you focused on, you've got to decide to be an activist.

How much did the presidents actually know about the keys? As noted earlier in this book, Clinton used the Lichtman keys (without crediting them) in response to a question in 1991 about whether he was going to run for president. By the time the second Bush became president, there was no point in even asking if Karl Rove was familiar with the keys. He's a big reader who loves big political ideas. The keys got attention in *The Washington Post,* and Lichtman's books got reviewed in political magazines. It's a subject that grabs political professionals. Rove knew. (Also, of course, the second Bush knew about the first Bush.)

That's about all I can offer as evidence that the keys have been dramatically influential. I have made no effort to question the presidents on their motives. I'm guessing they wouldn't tell me that the reason they enacted certain collections of policies was to get re-elected.

CHAPTER

12

Extrapolations: Lessons to be Drawn

Once you imbibe the logic of the keys, you find yourself rethinking everything. Is the world really round, just because the experts say it is? Well, maybe not everything. But you develop a skepticism of experts as a class that goes beyond the normal level of skepticism that everybody seems to give lip service to. You find yourself genuinely not caring whether the economic experts think the price of gasoline is going to rise more before it falls, whether the foreign-policy experts think Slobodan Milosevic will relent to NATO's bombing or the people of Iraq will welcome the Americans as liberators, or whether the education experts think vouchers or charter schools will work.

Well, we are not going to challenge everything. But, starting here, we move beyond the keys and, in some measure, beyond Lichtman to take a critical look at some of the shibboleths of politics whose acceptance is almost as universal as the obsession with campaigns and image manipulation. Some of the points made here are elaborations on points about the keys; and some have been made briefly in preceding sections. Others are new. Unleashed from conventional wisdom, we all become dangerous.

First of all,

All Politics Is Not Local

Lexis-Nexis is a computerized collection of the old and recent contents of major and minor newspapers and magazines. If, around the turn of the century, you did a search for the phrase "All politics is local," in combination with the name Tip O'Neill, late speaker of the U.S. House of Representatives, you got back a notice that the search could not be completed because it found more than 1,000 matches (including duplicate listings, in that the same article will appear in more than one publication). If you limited the search to two years and you left out any reference to O'Neill, you were still above the 1,000 threshold.

Speaker O'Neill was not the first to make the point that all politics is local, but he seems to have done more damage with it than anybody else.

You know the idea: Washington may get all caught up in grand debates about momentous issues or in petty squabbles over jurisdictional turf, but back home the focus is entirely different. Back home, the Washington personalities are seen differently from their images in Washington, and elections are fought over matters outside Washington's parochial vision.

The survival of this shibboleth is simply phenomenal.

If all politics is local—or nearly all, if any possible interpretation of the maxim survives, no matter how aggressively watered down—then the Republican tidal wave of 1994 was what? a coincidence?

Did it just so happen that all the best candidates were in the same party all of a sudden, and that all the crucial local issues happened to favor that party—but just for that year?

The truth about 1994 is that the party that tried to make the congressional elections local—the Democrats—failed. Let's not talk about Clinton and health care and all that, they said, in races across the country; let's talk about what I've done for this community. House Speaker Tom Foley was the classic example; he had done much for his district, through his exceptional power. The public didn't want to hear it. He lost.

Meanwhile, the party that tried to make the elections national—the Republicans, with Newt Gingrich's "Contract with America"—won.

The entire political community is familiar with at least one historical pattern in politics: the president's party usually loses House seats in midterm elections (the last two being exceptions). If all politics were local, that pattern wouldn't be there. There'd be no national pattern.

The all-politics-is-local shibboleth has a sub-shibboleth: presidential elections aren't one big election, but 50 small ones. Also wrong.

In 1980, Gallup issued a poll on the weekend before the presidential election saying the race was too close to call. In the end, however, the race was not close. Reagan got 51 percent of the vote, Carter 42 and John Anderson 7. The explanation for the contradiction is not that Gallup doesn't know how to take a poll. Last-minute, pre-election polls are a mastered technique. The demonstrated ability of the pollsters to do them—to often predict the outcomes of elections before the actual vote—is probably the reason for the political community's fascination with other types of polls, which are often far more dubious.

But some elections are more problematic than others. The 1980 election pitted an incumbent president on whose watch things had gone badly against a former actor of suspiciously immoderate views. People—that is, the swing voters who decide the outcome of our elections—wanted a change, but they weren't sure Ronald Reagan was a respectable one. If the Republican candidate had been Howard Baker or George Bush, the election would have been over in September. But people seemed to be waiting to see if Reagan would make that one gigantic mistake that would confirm the charge that he was just a nutball actor doing make-believe. The odds against that happening were huge, and it didn't. In the end, the change-seeking voters held their breath and cast their vote for the notion that the United States should not accept excuses for slow deterioration unless it absolutely has no choice.

Though Reagan's 55 percent of the two-party popular vote was substantial, his Electoral College victory was overwhelming: 91 percent. That means his victory—and the last-minute tide for him—was thoroughly national. He won by moderate amounts in states across the nation. It didn't depend on whether some local politicians could deliver votes better than others, or on who was on the ballot with Reagan, or on local issues.

As a general rule, all presidential politics is national. That's why, as noted earlier, Electoral College victories in modern elections have generally been bigger—usually much bigger—than popular-vote victories. Yes, 2000 was the exception. When an election comes down to one state, and the outcome there is a virtual tie, yes, of course, one must look at how local factors figured in. But, as noted earlier, the late polls consistently and overwhelmingly favored George W. Bush. The closeness of the election resulted from a last-minute mini-tide in favor of Al Gore, a mini-tide that swept the nation.

Statehouse Wins Don't Lead a Party to the Presidency

In the spirit of this book, here's a prediction:

The next time there's a midterm election, the people reporting and explaining the returns for the television networks will relate the outcomes of gubernatorial elections of that day to the presidential election two years hence. They will say that Democratic gains made today bode well for the party's hopes of regaining the presidency; or that Republican gains will help that party in the big one. The network people always do this. It is apparently in their contracts. Otherwise, surely, they would rebel. They would look at the record, an effort that takes five minutes, and they would say, "Wait a minute. We can't say that. That's demonstrably untrue."

Dan Rather, on Election Night, 1994: "In the governors' races—and if you think they aren't important, you are wrong, because for the 1996 presidential campaign, anybody who controls the state from the Statehouse really helps his presidential candidate...."

The statement, typical of many by anchors and lessers alike, is worth noting because it suggests that Rather couldn't think of any reason people should be interested in state politics other than its connection to national politics. For our purposes, though, the point is that he was wrong.

In 1982, the Democrats gained seven governorships; the Republicans dropping from 23 to 16. But the Democrats lost the 1984 presidential election. (More than 30 states had Democratic governors; one of those states voted Democratic in the presidential election.)

In the next midterm, 1986, Republicans gained eight governorships. They won the next presidential election.

In 1990, the Democrats lost one governorship. They won the next presidential.

In 1994, the GOP gained 11 governorships, taking a majority of states for the first time since 1970. And, as was often noted at the time, the party gained big states: New York and Texas, which together with the already-held California, Illinois, Ohio, Michigan, and Pennsylvania, put them in charge of nearly all the states where huge numbers of people actually live. Surely that would mean something for the next presidential election. But the party lost that election.

That's three out of four midterms in which the party that gained governorships turned out to lose the next presidential election. (Let us not pause over the 1998 midterms, because the outcome of the subsequent presidential election was so murky.)

You would think that the network pundits would have started reporting gubernatorial success as a danger sign. One need not do sophisticated computer analysis to unearth this pattern. One just needs to exercise due diligence. The networks have the resources.

To guess that a link might exist between gubernatorial and presidential elections is reasonable enough. After all, Lichtman has a link between House midterm elections and the next presidential. But his theory doesn't suggest that House members exercise some influence in presidential elections, only that their elections—in campaigns about national concerns—say something about the direction the country is going.

Rather's notion—or, really, everybody in networkdom's notion—that governors exercise some influence in presidential elections should be paused over. To the eye of someone who has followed local and state politics in one important and, by all accounts, typical state—Ohio—the idea is simply amazing. It appears to be about some other country.

The Democrats won the governorship of Ohio in 1982, then lost the presidential elections statewide in 1984 and 1988, despite retaining the governorship in 1986. They lost the governorship in 1990, then carried the state in the presidential elections in 1992 and 1996, despite losing the governorship again in 1994 (and 1998).

More important, there is not a single political observer in Ohio who sees anything the tiniest bit interesting or surprising about the fact that the governors have had no impact on the presidential elections. It is a fact that goes unremarked, because it is completely unremarkable. A governor, after all, has no mechanism with which to affect the outcome of a presidential election. He has no patronage employees around the state whom he can send door to door. To the degree he has promises he can make to voting blocs in return for their support, he is going to save them for his own election. No governor in Ohio in two decades has used any political capital to get a presidential candidate elected or taken anything close to a political risk for one.

A governor might have a role to play in a presidential primary. Various governors—including Ohio's Bob Taft—got behind Gov. George W. Bush in 2000 and seemed to play a role in convincing the party's voters—in this non-rebellious year—that he was the party's best bet.

But the notion that Independents or members of the other party are going to take some interest in the fact that a governor endorses the candidate of his own party in the general election is foreign to American experience. Most likely, no voter in two decades has paid any attention to anything like that. Governors aren't heroes, just politicians. And even if they were heroes, they couldn't transfer their popularity up the ballot to anybody else. Dwight Eisenhower and Ronald Reagan couldn't transfer their popularity down to anybody else (couldn't even keep their parties from backsliding in Congress during their presidencies). How could a governor transfer his popularity up? If anybody in modern Ohio politics could have done something like that, it would have been the only hero, John Glenn. But Glenn could just get himself elected to the Senate; nobody else, ever, to anything.

Among the top network people, the prevailing lack of feel for the nature of state and local politics is amazing and appalling.

Exit Polls Are Bunk, Even When Right

On the subject of Election Nights and the networks, the main point that must be made is that exit polls are bunk, and not because they can predict the wrong winner, as they did in 2004.

Exit polls are the exercises—engaged in by nearly all the networks, if not all—whereby a voter is confronted by a pollster after voting. The resulting polls had a good record before 2004 at telling who won. Respondents do generally seem to tell the pollsters the truth about whom they voted for; and extrapolation from the few who are polled to the many who are not is close to a mastered technique. This is why the networks can generally tell you who won a state as soon as the voting stops (which is as soon as custom will allow; the networks don't want to be accused of deterring people from voting by announcing results while the polls are open). Occasionally the networks do have to pull back from a "projection" (misleading word; sometimes they are not so much projecting from small returns as telling you the results of their polls), but not often.

This is one reason the exit pollsters have license to try to tell you why people voted as they did. If the pollsters are such wizards, the thinking seems to be, let's put them on the last remaining question: why.

But the pollsters are not up to the task. Going from figuring out what people did—pushed a pin into a certain spot, pushed a button, whatever—to why is not like going from A to B. The latter task is a far more complicated, treacherous one.

The exit pollsters asked people in the 1996 election whether they thought character or the economy was the more important issue. The results showed that people who chose character were more likely to vote for Bob Dole, and that people who chose the economy were more likely to vote for Bill Clinton.

Duh.

Then the pollsters tried to tell you that Dole's problem was that people were more concerned about the economy than character.

Similarly, in 1992, Bill Clinton got higher marks than George Bush on the "cares-about-people-like-me" scale, but Bush was rated better at dealing with foreign adversaries. So, the pundits decided, Bush's problem was that people just weren't all that concerned about foreign policy.

In the 2000 GOP primaries, people who voted for Sen. John McCain over Gov. George W. Bush generally said they were very concerned about campaign finance issues, and Bush voters said they weren't. Ergo, McCain's problem was that not enough people were focused on that issue.

But the case for each analysis is uncompelling.

For one thing, if you ask your questions immediately after a person has voted, you invite that person to offer answers that justify the vote.

If, say, arbitrarily, a soccer mom has just gone for Clinton, and she comes out, and a guy asks her whether she is more concerned with presidential character or the state of the economy, she is likely to say the economy. Life is easier for her if she says the economy. She doesn't have to worry about a follow-up question along the lines of, if you think character is the issue, how could you vote for Clinton? Likewise, if she voted for Dole in 1996 or Bush in 1992, she is not likely to say the economy is her chief concern. She knows that if she says that, she's got some explaining to do. (In fact, the number of people who don't give the pollsters the easy, obvious answers—who vote for Clinton and say their chief concern is character—may be roughly the number who don't have a clue what the issues are.)

Similarly, if the pollsters ask, as they did in 1996, a voter's views about the appropriate age of presidents, and they find, as they did, that Clinton voters are more likely to be concerned about Dole's relatively advanced age than Dole voters, they really haven't found that Dole's age hurt him. Nor if they find that Clinton voters were more likely to dislike Dole's views on taxes have they found that Dole's view hurt him.

Human motivation is a tricky and complicated thing. If you try to figure out what voters' motives are by asking them, you are assuming that they know and are willing to say, honestly.

If the questions you ask are multiple-choice—as they must be for a poll to be reported that night—you assume that the pollster has figured out the possible motivations and can put them into question form.

If you require a neat, simple answer, you are assuming that motivations are neat and simple, rather than the result of inchoate feelings and hunches.

Nobody is going to find out very much about voter motivations casually and quickly. Fortunately, in politics there is a better way than asking people about their motivations with simple, closed-ended questions in a setting that skews the results: you can look at the outcomes of many elections over a long period and then ask what characteristics the winners have in common. That—looking at what voters actually opt for under a broad range of circumstances—will suggest a lot about motivation.

There's No Such Thing as Coattails—Ever

The notion that a presidential candidate might have "coattails"—that is, might win by such a large margin that he carries other candidates of his party into office with him—is prevalent these days largely because of Ronald Reagan. When Reagan was elected president, so were a net of eight new GOP senators and 33 House members. No other presidential election has seen anything like that in the last third of a century. Generally, the big, sudden changes in Congress have occurred in midterm elections.

Bob Dole, in a speech on Capitol Hill in the spring of 2000, offered the conventional interpretation of GOP gains in 1980: "Ronald Reagan proved the experts wrong (about the GOP's minority status in the Senate being permanent) and his coattails gave Republicans a Senate majority for the first time in a quarter century."

The notion that Ronald Reagan had national coattails in 1980 is enshrined in political folklore; it's a given. The authoritative *National Journal* magazine referred as recently as May 6, 2000 to "a half-dozen of the GOP Senators who were swept in on Ronald Reagan's coattails in 1980."

It's strange. We are, after all, not talking about the year—1984—when Reagan won by a landslide. (Nothing much changed in Congress that year.) We're talking about the year—1980—when he won a popular vote victory that was just average in size: about nine percentage points over the Democrat. Why would we attribute coattails to such a modest victory?

The question becomes all the more interesting when you contemplate this: 1980 was a three-way race. John Anderson got seven percent of the vote. So Reagan's nine-point margin over Walter Mondale was achieved with 51 percent of the popular vote.

How does a coattails effect set in when a candidate gets 51 percent of the vote, and almost all his party's candidates lower down on the ballot are in two-way races and generally winning with higher percentages?

In reality, 1980 was not a Reagan phenomenon, but simply an excellent Republican year. Things were going badly for the country. It had recently experienced double-digit inflation, double-digit interest rates, gas shortages, the hostage taking in Iran and more. The party that controlled the presidency and both houses of Congress was paying a price. One does not need a reference to Ronald Reagan's magic to explain this; it was business as usual for the American political process.

And it would have happened with Howard Baker or George Bush at the top of the Republican ticket. Indeed, if one of them had been the nominee, John Anderson might not have seen an opening in the ideological center and might not have run. In that case, the GOP would have had higher percentages of the presidential vote. Making this case that the

Senate turnover was not a result of "Baker's coattails" would not have been quite so easy.

(By the way, Reagan's 51 percent is worth remembering the next time you hear the phrase "Reagan Democrat." It's a highly dubious phrase. A candidate need not get votes from members of the other party to get 51 percent of the total; there are more than enough Independents. True, Reagan got a lot more votes in 1984, but the term "Reagan Democrat" is not needed to explain a re-election landslide in good times. Actually, you don't need to draw from the other party to get a 60-percent landslide, either; you just need to sweep the swing voters.)

Why should anybody care whether the phenomenon at work is coattails or just a good year for a party? The answer is that what's at stake is an understanding of how American elections work.

Before the 2000 election, we were all becoming accustomed to the notion that the parties don't have the role in American life that they used to have. More and more people were calling themselves Independents. It was the fashionable thing to do. They'd say, "I don't vote for the party; I vote for the person." And the people who talked like that got a lot of attention.

Since 2000, one hears less talk about independence and more to the effect that the partisan standoff is narrow. That view is difficult to square with the notion that nobody cares about parties anymore. In fact, though, even before 2000, every indication was that—self-assigned labels notwithstanding—the vast majority of people voted regularly for a certain party, at least in two-way races.

After all, we call it a landslide when a race comes out 60-40 in percentages, or even a bit closer. But what those candidates with 40 are doing is getting their party's base. Often with no money, no respect in the media or the political community for their chances, no credentials to put up against an incumbent, they still manage to get an awful lot of votes. It's hard to imagine where those votes come from if not primarily from people who are very strongly predisposed toward the party.

And as for the people who are not voting for the same party almost all the time, even they seem to be voting with party in mind. The fact that their party selection in a given contest can often be predicted suggests that they are paying some attention to the concept of party. They just seem to think less in terms of the Democratic and Republican parties—and less in terms of "the person"—than in terms of the Incumbent and Challenging parties.

Before 1980, the last time a president was generally seen to have had coattails was 1964, when Barry Goldwater failed to carry any states except his own and some in the deep South in the presidential election against Lyndon Johnson. Johnson got about 60 percent of the popular vote. The Democrats, starting with a sizable majority in the House, gained almost 40 seats, to arrive at a dominating 295 total, out of 435.

To see 1964 as a coattails phenomenon—or even as an anti-Goldwater phenomenon—is to see something programmatic, something ideological in the votes of the Independents. It's possible. Maybe some people were just so appalled at Goldwater that they were appalled that any party would nominate him, and they saw a danger in any votes for that party.

But only about 55 percent of all white voters voted for Johnson. What made the election a landslide was that blacks were virtually unanimous against Goldwater, who opposed the landmark Civil Rights Act of 1964 (granting equal access to public accommodations, such as restaurants and stores). These were the years when civil rights emerged as a central issue, and when black Americans as a group completed their migration from the party of Abraham Lincoln to the Democrats. And they turned out to vote, at least in the North, where there were no barriers to voting.

A theory is emerging that the turnout issue is someplace near the center of elections in which one party dominates. For example, the theory holds, what happened in 1980 and 1994 was not so much a matter of Independent voters going down the line for Republicans, as it was a matter of Republican-leaning voters being energized and Democratic-leaning voters being demoralized and not voting. It's difficult to measure convincingly, because many factors seem to influence a decision to vote or not. But the theory makes some sense.

If the turnout theory is right, then the coattails theory is wrong.

At any rate, the coattails idea dates from a time when people could cast a party-line vote by checking one square at the top of a paper ballot or, later, flipping one lever. That option prevailed in many states in 1964. Under those circumstances, having a popular figure at the top of a ticket certainly did work to the advantage of a party.

Even back then, however, the idea of Democratic years and

Republican years explains a lot more than the idea of coattails for individuals. In the 1890 midterm election—that is, an election with no popular presidential candidate at the top of the ballot—the Democrats gained 75 House seats. In the next midterm, 1894, they lost 116. These vast fluctuations seem to suggest that it was either one party's year (nationally) or the other's.

The notion of coattails suggests that there are times when the voters want to give a president a like-minded Congress. However, given how frequently the voters choose to undermine a president's power in midterm elections, it seems unlikely that they are highly motivated to concentrate power in his hands in presidential elections.

The coattails idea will not die. In 2004, the media and the politicians will once again be discussing the chances of some candidate to bring his party to dominance in Congress. (Historical patterns make that prediction easy.) But, in a time when ballots are designed to minimize the visibility of party—when a party's candidates appear first in some races and third in others—the prospect of swing voters going through a ballot looking for the candidates of one party because they like that party's presidential candidate is hard to imagine. The partisan majority, yes; the decisive swing voters, no.

Name Recognition Isn't the Point

In the days before a political campaign, you often hear a lot of talk about how a political party is looking for a candidate with strong name recognition. This is presumed to be an advantage in a general election. So actors get talked about as possible candidates, as do athletes and people from prominent families; or even people who just happen to have famous names, even if neither they nor their family members are actually famous. For similar reasons, former candidates also get considered, as do former officeholders. Or anybody who has made a lot of news: the police chief or school superintendent, for example.

And, the thinking often goes, if we can't find somebody with high name recognition, then let's find somebody who has enough money to buy name recognition.

The notion that voters are more likely to pick somebody whose name they recognize has something to be said for it. In races for low-level offices, one candidate frequently has an advantage in name recognition. That candidate is likely to win, or at least do better than his party is normally expected to do.

Moreover, the party leaders who are seeking candidates who have high name recognition don't generally get stupid about it. They are not likely to recruit Dennis Rodman or Pee Wee Herman. Nor would they be likely to be enthusiastic about the political aspirations of a latter-day namesake of Adolf Hitler. Actually, they probably wouldn't want anybody named Hitler or Adolf.

Jerry Springer—talk show host to the appalling—was put forth as a possible candidate for the U.S. Senate in Ohio in 2000 and 2004. His first promoter was the Democratic Party chairman in Hamilton County (Cincinnati). Springer had been mayor of Cincinnati (getting the job by receiving more votes for the city council than anybody else) and had run for the party nomination for governor in 1982. But the Senate idea was met both times with widespread disgust and a heated debate in political circles about whether he'd be a strong candidate. In 2003, Springer clearly wanted to run in 2004; he campaigned for months. But he found that he could not change the fact that his reputation was negative. And he decided not go through with it.

Some politicians know that the concept they are dealing with is not exactly name recognition, but, rather, positive name recognition, or at least non-negative.

Even at that, though, they are missing something: at the end of a long, hard campaign for a high-profile office—mayor, governor, senator—both candidates in a general election have all the name recognition they need. The people who vote are the kind who have heard of the candidates for the highest offices.

Major advantages in name recognition can be overcome in a campaign. In Minnesota in 1990, Democratic Senate candidate Paul Wellstone had a name recognition percentage in the 30s at the start of the campaign. But, with no extraordinary amount of money, he managed to defeat incumbent Sen. Rudy Boschwitz. The name recognition comes if the candidacy has a shot.

Polls taken in mid-September often find nearly 100-percent name recognition for candidates for major statewide office. And that's before the media blitz starts. All Americans are familiar with the concept of instant fame. It happens all the time to people who become the objects of intense media attention. Well, the media really do get serious about politics in October. They can make anybody famous—however briefly.

True, the candidate's name may be widely forgotten by the next spring. In the book *What Americans Know about Politics* (Yale University Press, 1996), Michael X. Delli Carpini and Scott Keeter report that only 25 percent of Americans can name both their senators. A U.S. senator's 15 minutes of fame sometimes ends when he takes office.

Whatever the name-recognition situation in November, the possibility ought to be pondered that there is some advantage to being known before the campaign. Maybe being known gives voters a certain comfort level with a candidate. Almost certainly, that is true of candidates who are known for political activity. Many are the politicians who lost several races before winning any. Newt Gingrich won a congressional seat only on his third attempt. Sen. William Proxmire had to try repeatedly, but is now known in Wisconsin as a man of legendary popularity. (He eventually started winning re-elections without spending any money.) In Ohio, all the U.S. senators elected during the last quarter century—Howard Metzenbaum, John Glenn, George Voinovich and Mike DeWine—have lost Senate races (primaries or generals) before winning. Two of the last three governors (Dick Celeste and George Voinovich) have also lost statewide races first.

So, yes, a certain kind of pre-campaign name recognition is useful.

But the litany of well-recognized people who have failed politically is long. All Americans are familiar with actors and athletes who have succeeded. (And a professional wrestler, whichever category you want to put him in.) But the names of failures are forgotten. Ernie Banks, as big a hero in Chicago as his era ever saw, ran for the city council as a Republican and got swamped. Warren Beatty didn't exactly light a national fire when he flirted very publicly with running for president in 2000. Richard Petty, the race-car driver, ran for secretary of state in North Carolina, starting with 95-percent name recognition, and lost. John Gavin, a movie heartthrob in his time, failed to generate any interest for a Senate race in 1986, despite having a credential as former ambassador to

Mexico. Actor Ben Jones, from a television show that was supposed to be particularly popular in the South (*The Dukes of Hazzard*), failed to turn his celebrity into success against Newt Gingrich in multiple races. He did manage to get to Congress eventually, after building name recognition as a political figure.

The Arnold Schwarzenegger phenomenon in California's 2003 gubernatorial recall will certainly fuel the widespread fascination with celebrity and name recognition as political forces. But that was an extraordinary set of circumstances.

For the famous and not-famous alike, the circumstances have to be right. And the best guideline—relating to the normal course of things, not California in 2003—is that, once you get a nomination, the circumstances are right about half the time. (That is, of the two candidates, one has to win.)

As for getting a nomination, pre-campaign name recognition may, indeed, be useful. The best generalization may be the same one to be made about money: it's more useful in primaries. Primaries tend not to involve philosophical distinctions that automatically divide most of the electorate into two camps, leaving only swing voters to fight over. The absence of ideology and incumbent performance as dominant factors may leave more room for the name-recognition factor to operate. This is particularly true in low-visibility races, which primaries tend to be.

To use another Ohio example, the Democratic Senate primary in 2000 came down to three people, none of whom was well known before the race. One was the brother of former Gov. Dick Celeste. The other two were not, though their qualifications were at least as good, if not better. Celeste won easily. This was unmistakably a name-recognition phenomenon.

But Celeste got blown away in the general, failing even to make it interesting against Sen. Mike DeWine, no great powerhouse as a candidate.

One more note on name recognition: Gov. George W. Bush was leading Al Gore in the presidential polls as early as mid-1999, when, most certainly, most Americans did not know what he did for a living. He did not have a high national profile as the governor of Texas. In the polls, some sort of mix-up was at work between him and his father; or maybe the name was enough for people at that stage. At any rate, he was the only Republican leading Gore, and the Republicans who were looking for somebody to beat Gore didn't ask any questions. They piled on a poll-created bandwagon. (Gov. Bush himself was moved by the polls; asked at one stage what made him think about running, he said he hadn't thought about it until he saw himself leading in the polls.)

In the end, though, Bush was not a better candidate in the fall because of his name. The notion that he would be is odd; after all, former President George Bush is hardly a national icon. But George W. Bush wasn't bad either, despite the charge that he lacked depth and experience, especially in foreign policy. Getting the nomination of a major party for president provides all the name recognition and respect a candidate needs. If the candidate was obscure beforehand, it doesn't matter; ask Jimmy Carter or Bill Clinton. If he had national name recognition beforehand, it doesn't matter; ask Bob Dole or Walter Mondale. What matters is the year.

The Issues Are Not the Issue

In the first version of this book that existed in my imagination, the central point wasn't going to be that the importance of campaigns is generally grossly overestimated, but that the importance of ideology is. The book was going to argue that elections are not about who's most in tune with the views of the public. It would hold that words like liberal and conservative don't explain much.

These days that point hardly needs to be made. When the Democrats win control of the presidency one year, 1992 (while holding both houses of Congress), and the Republicans take over Congress in the next election, and the Democrats breeze back into the White House in the next, and the next is a tie (with one party winning under one set of rules, and the other under other rules), and Congress settles into seemingly permanent near-equality for the parties, it is not hard to convince people that ideology is not very useful as an explanation of election outcomes.

Not long ago, however, the conventional view was that the conservatives were on the march. The view derived from Republican dominance of presidential elections. The GOP won five out of six from 1968 through, let's say, 1991. Two of their wins were landslides; their only loss came after Watergate; it was paper-thin; and it was to Jimmy Carter, who, some

Republicans said, could only fool the people into thinking he wasn't a liberal for so long.

For a huge number of commentators, this record constituted sufficient proof that the Republicans had the more popular views. Commentator George Will made this point more times than anybody should make any point. Actually, the view hardly got disputed. The liberals were often reduced to pointing out that most people don't vote in midterms, and almost half don't vote in presidentials. So it wasn't the people the GOP was doing well with, only the voters. Some Democrats apparently found some comfort in that.

The fact that the Democrats continued to control both houses of Congress through this period posed no analytical challenge to the conventional wisdom. The most common explanation was incumbency: the Democrats controlled Congress because the Democrats controlled Congress. After all, the 1980s were the years when incumbent House members of both parties won re-election races so regularly—at rates well above 90 percent—that the term-limits movement was born as the only apparent recourse against them.

In fact, however, in the two decades before the 1994 GOP takeover of the House, the Republican Party had won more than enough seats for a majority. It had defeated Democratic incumbents 86 times, and it had won open seats that were being vacated by Democrats 48 times. It just never had enough seats at any given time. This was because, when its members voluntarily vacated seats (usually in pursuit of higher office), the party lost 44 seats; and 64 of its incumbents had been beaten. So the Democrats did not have to be incumbents to win.

(Judging from the popularity of the term-limits movement, the general public seemed to think the House was full of 20- or 30-year veterans. That was never close to true. Members were always moving on voluntarily. Between 11 and 17 percent had 20 years of seniority, depending on what year you look at, according to the American Enterprise Institute book *Vital Statistics on Congress – 1997-1998,* which is also the source of the numbers in the previous paragraph.)

One theory about why Republicans did better in those years' presidential elections than congressional ones came from well-known pundit Ben Wattenberg. He said that the higher the office, the more ideology matters to voters.

Another, noted earlier, was that the public wanted one kind of president (tough, especially in foreign policy), and another kind of Congress (generous).

For both theories, Republican dominance of the presidency resulted from the party's ideology.

Then, in the 1990s, everything changed. The parties exchanged the presidency and Congress. Surprisingly enough, this did not cause the people who had seen ideology as the explanation for Republican dominance of the presidency to start saying they were wrong. They could still find ways to say what they wanted to believe. That is trivially easy in politics. They could say that the Democrats came in from the left in 1992 (a dubious notion, when one looks at their 1988 posture, as has been noted elsewhere in this book). They could say that foreign policy ceased to be an intense concern for voters (though that had pretty much happened by 1988). Whatever.

But the necessity to scramble to come up with something could be avoided. They could accept the notion inherent in the Lichtman keys: that the Democrats' problem during that 5-1 GOP hot streak was not public revulsion at allegedly excessive liberalism; it was that Democratic presidencies were ending quite badly, and most Republican presidencies were ending rather well.

One wouldn't expect partisan Republicans to have great difficulty embracing this view.

In 1968, the Democrats lost the presidency because the country and the party seemed to be coming apart at the seams, while the nation was bogged down in a dubious war. They lost it again, after only one term, in 1980 because the party was divided again (between Jimmy Carter and Ted Kennedy) in the face of a tough economy, international humiliation (in Iran) and a general national sense of a lack of presidential leadership.

Meanwhile, in that '68-'88 period, the Republicans won re-election three times, because things were either not so bad or pretty darn good. So Democratic critics of Republican administrations couldn't get the kind of traction with non-partisan voters that Republican critics of Democratic administrations were able to get.

Now, if one wants to make the case that the Democrats' liberalism was the reason their presidencies were not working out, fine. That's another book. For what it's worth, liberalism wasn't the explanation for Vietnam. And even the Republican partisans would have to grant that one factor that affects the outcomes of presidencies is luck (otherwise they can't explain Clinton). But let's not have that fight right now. It can be saved for a time when the keys gain more currency, when the old disputes within the political-analysis class are seen as irrelevant, and the old-school advocates decide to join in the new discussion.

The Votes Are Not "At the Center"

"GOP Right Accepts Bush's Move to Middle," reads a *Washington Post* headline of May 27, 2000. "Convinced that he is committed to their core issues—tax cuts, opposition to abortion, and personal values—and recognizing that the formula they adopted in the mid-1990s will not win the White House," the story says, "these conservatives are willing to back Bush even if he spends much of the presidential campaign focused on traditionally Democratic themes."

The votes are in the center, one has often heard during various political periods. One didn't hear it often in 1994. Or when Ronald Reagan was winning the presidency easily. Or during the early years of this century, when voters were widely seen as more "polarized" than they had been for decades. But the notion is typically dominant and has never completely gone away. Most typically, it is stated that baldly: "The votes are in the center." Not in the center "these days." Just in the center, as if it's an immutable rule of politics.

It has never been anything close. And yet the center can't be ignored. (So what we have here is a centrist position on the role of the center.)

A little history: When Barry Goldwater ("Extremism in defense of liberty is no vice") was seeking the Republican presidential nomination of 1964, the party had a great big fight about whether the votes were in the center. Goldwater insisted that millions of people would vote for him who otherwise wouldn't vote at all, because they had no use for the moderates and liberals they were generally confronted with. But he got blown away in a 60-40 general-election landslide, and the party came back toward the center. Then, in 1972, the Democrats abandoned the center, nominating George McGovern, who wanted to pull out of Vietnam instantaneously, slash defense spending by $30 billion and (this is true) give everybody $1,000, which was a lot more money back then. They got blown away in a 60-40 landslide, and the party came back to the center.

After that, it was hardly worth arguing about whether the votes were in the center.

But along came Ronald Reagan. He called upon the Republican Party to abandon the center in pursuit of principle. He rejected detente with the Soviet Union, a creation of his own party. He called for a massive tax cut in the face of a massive deficit, eliciting the "voodoo economics" charge from George H.W. Bush, exactly the kind of person Reagan was calling upon the party to reject. The 1976 fight between the Gerald Ford moderates and the Ronald Reagan non-moderates within the party was bitter and intense. It was seen as a fight over the soul of the party.

In 1980, the Democrats were hoping that the nominee would be Reagan. The March 31 *Newsweek* reported that they had, before that month, considered him "an easy mark." They were—need it be said—reading the polls. They revised their view when March polls showed a dead heat. But polls continued to show other Republican candidates doing better than Reagan against Carter. As Reagan moved toward clinching the nomination, former President Ford spoke up, saying, according to an Associated Press story of March 10, that the party could not win the presidency with Reagan at the top of the ticket. (Howard Baker had been the early choice of the party professionals, precisely because he was seen as more moderate and, therefore, more electable.)

Reagan won the presidency easily. Some might consider that an exception to the votes-are-at-the-center rule, resulting from the fact that 1980 was such a bad year that people were open to the extremes, and from his exceptional charisma. He won much bigger in 1984, in much better times. Even that could be written off as an incumbency phenomenon abetted by charisma.

But after a while there are too many exceptions for the rule to have much life.

If the votes are at the center, why was national microcosm Illinois electing Reagan and true-blue liberal Sen. Paul Simon through the 1980s? Why was the microcosm state of Ohio electing both Ronald Reagan and true-blue liberal Sen. Howard Metzenbaum?

Why was the Newt Gingrich effort able to thrive in the early 1990s? Like Reagan, he was explicitly calling upon the Republican Party to reject the ways of moderation, as embodied by previous generations of House Republican leaders, such as Bob Michel. In Gingrich we had a man who, after the 1994 election, explicitly and repeatedly said he would not compromise on policy. "Cooperate, yes; compromise no," he said, meaning apparently that he was willing to discuss House schedules.

The Republicans have had one really great election in the House in the past 50 years, and that was the year Gingrich was at his peak of impact, when the House candidates were signing his "contract" and aping his ideological style. The freshmen of 1995 were universally seen as little Gingriches, only more so.

Meanwhile, of course, the Republican moderates who were running for governorships that year did well, too. But the point here is not that political victories are easier to achieve at the edges; only that they aren't necessarily easier at the center.

Ideology does have some impact. Barry Goldwater and George McGovern almost certainly lost some votes because the public perceived major forces in their own parties as finding them too extreme. That sort of thing sends a bad signal to Independents.

Nevertheless, the Republicans in 1964 and the Democrats in 1972 were going to lose by some margin or other. The elements for victory just weren't there. When they are there—as for the Republicans in 1980— somehow a candidate who rejects the party's moderate traditions manages to keep the coalition together. And if the coalition hangs together, in the end the only question the swing voter is left with is whether change is desirable.

After Bill Clinton's party suffered its monumental defeat in 1994, he tacked back to the center, and the party recovered with remarkable speed. The lesson some people draw is that the votes are at the center. Clinton probably did have to go to the center, for this reason alone: so many people in his own party were convinced that he had to—especially southerners in

Congress—that if he had not done so, he might well have faced a potent challenge from within the party for renomination. And, as we have seen, that could have cost him the Lichtman key that is the single best predictor of victory and defeat of all the keys. The incumbent party cannot be seriously divided. And Clinton had no keys to spare.

Even with the general public though, Clinton did probably benefit from being seen as the moderate, down-to-earth antidote to Gingrich. Gingrich's immoderation worked a lot better when he didn't have power than when he did.

As the chapter in this book about 1994 noted, there are occasions upon which a party will pay a price in congressional elections for losing touch with the center. The Democrats probably pressed for too much change too fast when they found themselves with control of everything after 1992; and the Republicans probably pressed for too much after 1994.

Even in those cases, though, a sweeping generalization about the votes being at the center is dangerous. The Democrats who maintained centrist images had no more success than their liberal brethren. In Oklahoma, centrist Democratic Rep. Dave McCurdy, widely considered one of the rising stars of the party, lost his bid for an open Senate seat to uncompromising conservative Rep. James Inhofe. In Tennessee, Democrats lost two Senate seats, one involving centrist incumbent Jim Sasser and one with centrist Rep. Jim Cooper. Meanwhile, such liberal stalwarts as Ted Kennedy and New Jersey Sen. Frank Lautenberg did fine (as did some incumbent Democratic moderates, such as Chuck Robb).

A wise political leader does, of course, have a feel for what the market will bear ideologically. Ultimately, Newt Gingrich's movement collapsed not because he was too high-strung or weird, but because the country simply did not want any sort of "revolution." By the mid-1990s, the country was simply doing too well. Under any circumstances, if one were going to try to build a revolution, one would be better off to start with Democratic constituencies, meaning the poor. To start with Republican constituencies is to start with people who have too much to risk.

So Gingrich's ideology brought him down. But that was a highly unusual situation. In the normal run of things, in any given election, both candidates are solidly entrenched enough in the political mainstream that any contests between them are decided by other factors.

If, in accord with the conventional wisdom about where the votes are, a candidate moves to the center, there are likely to be down sides. For one thing, the political motivations of the move may be transparent. The candidate sets his opponent up to run those annoying "flip-flop" ads alleging that the candidate has no principles. Second, every time you move, you tick somebody off. Candidates like Ronald Reagan and Ted Kennedy demonstrate that there are advantages to sticking with the same people all the time: they stick with you, and that helps. They contribute money, drum up support, take your side when something you've said needs defending. No case is made here that these advantages are greater than those of moving to the center. The point is simply that there are trade-offs. These trade-offs will generally result in the ideology issue canceling itself out. Then the election outcome will be determined by something else. Therefore, what a candidate should think about is not which ideological posture will help, but—to stray here from centrism in political analysis—what he or she actually believes in.

Gender Gap, Schmender Gap

Those of us political types who came of age 30 years ago or more learned that men and women vote pretty much alike, that households tend to vote as households. The feminist movement that came alive at the end of the 1960s didn't seem to change that. But then, in the 1980s, the polls started showing decidedly less support for conservative Republican candidates among women than men. Maybe it was abortion; maybe it was that, as families broke up, more women than men found themselves in poverty; maybe it was that the Republicans had gone more conservative, while a certain liberal, feminist consciousness had set in among some types of women.

The media immediately took to referring to this "gender gap" in the polls as a problem for the Republicans. This makes little sense in a race in which the Republican is winning. If men are going in majority for the Republican, and women are going in the majority for Democrats, and, on balance, the Republican is ahead, then the phenomenon at work is that

Democrats are having a bigger problem with men than the Republicans are having with women.

But the gender gap was essentially promoted by feminist groups. They had a stake in it, because it suggested that, even if men were buying into this Reagan stuff, women weren't. And that suggested that the feminists were being heard by women, or were on their wavelength. It was natural for the media to see the polls as tests of feminism among women.

Eventually, however, the gender gap did come to be seen most often as a problem for the Democrats. This was because the 1994 polls showed white males, especially in the South, voting against Democrats in breathtaking proportions, with white women voting against Democrats in more modest numbers. That's a pretty difficult situation to spin into a problem for the Republicans.

And so the refrain went up: What can the Democrats do about their problem with white guys?

Stupid question.

The way for the party with the presidency to thrive in the long run is to govern well for the nation as a whole, and to have some luck. To approach the problem with specific demographic groups in mind is to risk getting involved in a zero-sum game. To think in terms of the white guys is to invite problems with non-white guys. There's always a backlash. The Democrats became the first to really reach out to blacks as blacks (rather than as poor people) in the 1960s, and it definitely got blacks, sometimes in numbers over 90 percent. But the party has been paying a price ever since, with blue-collar whites, Southerners and others.

The parties have sustained a rough equilibrium for decades now, each generally in control of part of the government. Even in the short periods when the Democrats have had the presidency and both houses of Congress, they generally didn't have philosophical control. In the 1960s, they generally only had majorities if you counted the Southern conservatives. Then, after Watergate, they had big majorities, but they had no sense that this fact meant the public was calling for a specific direction for the government. They were right, and they did almost nothing.

As this is written, the Republicans control everything in Washington, but their control of the Senate has, literally, no room to spare. So they are dependent on their few moderates, and have been able to move little of controversy besides tax cuts.

The reason for the equilibrium between the parties is partly that we have a competitive system in which neither side can catch the other by surprise. Nobody is likely to come up with sole possession of a great long-term stratagem, a gambit that doesn't involve a price to be paid.

Both parties are going to do badly with some demographic groups. To, after a bad election, define a party's overall problem as the problem with the most troublesome demographic group is to miss the point. What the Democrats needed to do after 1994 was improve with all major groups. Not carry them all, but improve with them all.

That didn't seem promising in 1994, because the country was already doing pretty well, with a strong economy, domestic peace and no great foreign crisis. One might have expected those factors to benefit the party with the presidency. But midterm elections have a different dynamic than presidential ones. In the end, a keys-based approach to 1996—that is, essentially, one built around incumbency and a successful economy, with a lack of trouble abroad—brought in a plurality of voters who belong to the good Democratic groups—women, poor people, blacks, union workers, academics, etc. It also brought in enough people from other groups to leave the pundits wondering whether they should go back to saying, "Boy, those Republicans really have a problem with women, don't they."

There Are No Anti-Incumbent Years

In congressional election outcomes, there are three kinds of years: Democratic, Republican and pro-incumbent. That is, either one party gains, or there's not much change. There are no anti-incumbent years, defined as incumbents of both parties having problems and losing in large numbers.

You don't hear political people talk much about anti-incumbent years, anymore. But the idea got much attention in the early 1990s. This contradiction was in the air: The public seemed generally dissatisfied with the way things were going in Washington and for the country. (In those years, Donald Bartlett and James Steele of *The Philadelphia Inquirer* won a Pulitzer Prize for a long series and a book called *America: What Went Wrong?* It was mainly an analysis of the economic problems besetting Americans.) But the politicians in Washington kept getting re-elected. This led to a certain uprising against the incumbents. This uprising—including the term-limits movement—got much attention. But not many House incumbents were ever defeated in general elections in any one year.

In 1986 and again in 1988—when the economy was doing better than in the early 1990s—only six House members were defeated in general elections. These were record lows. In 1990, the number was 15, still lower than most years. In 1992 it went to 24, about average over the past 50 years. And in 1994 it was 34, but, of course, that wasn't an anti-incumbent year, but an anti-Democratic one. Not a single Republican incumbent lost that year (in the Senate or in governorship races, either, for that matter).

The closest thing to an anti-incumbent year was 1992. It was the year of the House banking "scandal," in which scores of legislators of both parties were found to have been writing checks against insufficient funds in the House bank, and having the checks honored pending their next paycheck.

That year saw 19 House members defeated in primaries, the most in at least 50 years. In most years, that number is in single digits. In both 1988 and 1990, it was one.

Most unusual about 1992 was that 16 incumbent Democrats lost their seats to Republicans, and 8 Republicans lost theirs to Democrats, upsetting the general rule that losses tend to go in one direction.

Meanwhile, in general elections, the victory margins were diminishing for incumbents. Two-thirds of incumbents who won in 1992 got more than 60 percent of the vote. That sounds like a lot. But in 1990 three-fourths of the winners had been over 60 percent, and in 1988 and 1986 about 88 percent were. (The numbers again are from *Vital Statistics on Congress—1997-1998,* published by the American Enterprise Institute.)

So, yes, the anti-incumbent mood did have some effect. All the talk about the anti-incumbency wave may have fostered some challenges that otherwise might not have happened. That is, the alleged "mood" of the nation might have caused some people to see an opportunity—and some people to contribute to them and some media people to pay attention to them.

Even at that, though, 325 members were re-elected (most by landslides), coming to 88.3 percent of those who sought re-election. Those numbers were unusually low. But to call it an anti-incumbent year would be quite a stretch.

The anti-incumbent phenomenon wasn't enough, in the end, to upset the general pattern: come November, the public must have a particular party to blame, or it doesn't shake things up much.

CHAPTER

13

Ruminations: So What Does a Political Person Do?

If you embrace the ideas at the core of this book, you find yourself applying them to situations for which they were not intended.

In the 1980s, one of the great foreign-policy issues dividing Washington was Nicaragua. There a successful 1979 uprising against a right-wing dictator had produced a government that was getting aid from the Soviet Union and was being accused of moving repressively to the left. The Nicaraguan economy languished, heavy-handed Leninist tendencies engendered resentment, and anti-government uprisings arose outside the capital of Managua. Then, after the fall of the Soviet Union, the Sandinistas, apparently buckling to international and domestic pressure, moved toward a genuine election. It became a choice between them and an extraordinarily broad coalition of anti-Sandinistas, including many former Sandinistas.

The election was covered in momentous terms throughout the international media: Can a Marxist-influenced government hold power in a democracy? Or will a majority prefer capitalism and friendship with the United States?

But for a Lichtmaniac, the election did not seem to be a test of left vs. right. It seemed to be a test of whether a government could remain in power after a decade of economic decline, unending violence and bitter divisions within the governing party.

(Now, one might argue that the two ways of looking at the election are fundamentally the same, because a Marxist-leaning government almost inevitably produces phenomena like a bad economy, a guerrilla uprising and political splintering; but that's a different book.)

The logic of the keys suggested the Sandinistas should lose. That's what happened. This might not prove much. (As a matter of fact, though some people thought the anti-Sandinista coalition was too diverse and unwieldy to deliver a coherent message and that the Sandinistas would win because they were seen by the electorate as a force for vibrant nationalism). My point is simply about the way a Lichtman disciple thinks.

In 2006, a Palestinian election shook the world. To the surprise of everybody, the winning party was Hamas, known to the world as a terrorist organization. Some analysts on the scene tried to suggest that this was more a rejection of the futile Fatah government than an embrace of terrorism. A Lichtman disciple wasn't as skeptical as others might have been.

Even if you can't say the keys will predict Nicaraguan, Palestinian, gubernatorial or mayoral elections X percent of the time, you find yourself approaching those elections differently. When others start wondering who might be the strongest candidate against an incumbent governor a year hence, you find yourself thinking that they might as well not be asking, because nothing has gone wrong enough for the incumbent governor to lose. When others start listing the "issues" on which the governor might be vulnerable—abortion, school choice, taxes, whatever—because the voting majority seems to disagree with him, you find yourself lecturing them in your own mind or out loud about the irrelevance of such considerations. They start talking about the interest groups he has ticked off at the state capitol, and it sounds to you like so much insider hair-splitting. *You* know that it's big, generally-known things that affect the outcome of elections, not little, inside stuff.

But one must be careful. Lichtman took a shot at developing a scheme for gubernatorial races once, but he didn't get very far with it. He said at the time that he wasn't getting the kind of 90-percent success rate in looking at past races that he was with his Senate schemes. (An 80-percent success rate might interest some people; it did not interest him.)

He has not even tried to develop schemes in other kinds of elections.

Lichtman started his research with the belief that what the public wanted from presidents was successful performance as measured by some non-ideological, non-partisan standard. His research confirmed that. He started with the same view about Senate elections and was unable to confirm it. He came up instead with predictors that are more diffuse in their logic (though one might gather from thinking about them that the overriding consideration of the non-partisan public is senatorial stature). With regard to other kinds of races, the "key" factors may not be as simple as in presidential or senatorial races. Or as universal. For all anybody knows, people in Louisiana may expect different things of their governor than do people in New York.

Moreover, it is entirely possible that, with regard to other kinds of races—say for low-profile jobs at the state and local level—much of the conventional political wisdom is right. Maybe campaigns and name recognition and money and media manipulation and endorsements and envelope stuffing are, to one degree or another, where the meaningful action is.

In more than a decade of writing for newspapers about the ideas behind this book as they relate to presidential and Senate elections, I have found that many people simply don't want to believe this stuff, this general downplaying of campaign events, ideology, personality and other common grist for the pundit's mill. The reluctance comes from, among others, the political professionals. Not surprising; their alleged expertise is less important if the ideas presented here are accepted. The reluctance also comes from many seasoned political journalists. Also not surprising; they are being accused of having been wrong about so much for so long.

The reluctance also comes, however, from people who have no professional stake, people who just follow politics as citizens. They seem to feel that the ideas presented here threaten to take all or much of the fun out of politics. After all, if you know before a campaign who's going to be re-elected, what's the point of participating as a volunteer or of contributing money or of gathering around the television on election night?

Moreover, some people simply enjoy consuming the "horse-race" stuff the journalists produce about the day-to-day events of election campaigns and pre-campaign seasons. If Al Gore has some high-priced consultant telling him not to wear so much brown, they want to know about it. They like knowing about polls and campaign strategies and who's up and who's down within campaign teams. They'd prefer not to think it's all irrelevant.

With these concerns in mind, let's talk about what the ideas presented in this book do not—and, in some cases, do—amount to, for political junkies, for the politicians and their advisers, for the media, for members of the public who take their politics seriously, and, finally, for the democracy.

For Political Junkies

The first point that should be made is that the predictive schemes presented here don't always work. If the presidential scheme has always worked so far (a disputed point), it most assuredly will fail some day. The schemes provide a framework for looking at American electoral politics that, if the claims of the book hold up, is a lot better than the framework that is generally offered. But the book does not answer every question about the political future that can arise.

The Nicaraguan case notwithstanding, ingesting what this book has to offer does not result in political omniscience. I ingested years ago, and I have, nevertheless, been surprised by electoral developments in a fair range of races in recent years. In other races, I have simply had no strong sense of where things were going.

In 1998, when the Democrats became the first party with the presidency in memory to make gains in the U.S. House of Representatives in a midterm election, it surprised me as much as anyone. I didn't see any extraordinary events in play that seemed likely to upset the historical pattern. The last time the pattern didn't prevail was 1934. Nothing nearly so historic seemed in play in 1998 as the New Deal and the public's first chance to react to it—and its opponents—in an election. I could not accept the notion that Republican efforts to benefit from the Monica Lewinsky scandal (which broke at the beginning of 1998 and moved into impeachment at the beginning of 1999) would hurt the Republicans. Whatever one might think about the relevance or irrelevance of the Lewinsky matter, the notion that a scandal for one party might backfire on the other was just too at odds with historical precedent.

I also did not see the 1994 Republican tidal wave coming. I did not see

George W. Bush emerging as an unbeatable candidate for the Republican presidential nomination in 2000. I did not see Bill Bradley coming on as strong or fading as fast as he did against Al Gore in the 2000 primaries. At the local level, I've been right about some races, wrong about some and unable to make confident predictions in others.

I do not find politics any less fun because of what I believe about the Lichtman system. My focus is changed. Now much of the fun is in trying to figure out when and where the logic of the keys will hold. It's a different framework, a different, more accurate prism. That's all.

For Politicians and Their Supporters

Besides not answering all existing questions, the keys raise new ones. For example, what happens when the politicians start accepting the keys?

What if, say, in a particular presidential election, the keys say that the incumbents will win, but that if it weren't for a particular scandal—or a particular international defeat or economic problem—the challengers would win? Does the side that stands to lose decide that its job is to convince the public that the scandal didn't amount to much; or that the international situation is different than it looks at first glance?

And if a particular campaign does decide to take this keys-based tack, might it succeed?

Hard to say. The question becomes this: in a system that's based upon historical precedents, what happens when something unprecedented happens (i.e., the candidates start playing to the keys)? Lichtman anticipated this question; that's one reason he built his schemes upon many historical patterns, rather than one. But he is not under the delusion that he came up with a foolproof method of dealing with changing circumstances.

I am reduced to the answer I heaped contempt upon in earlier chapters, in another context: it all depends. In other words, I don't know.

The uncertainty ought to please those who complain that the keys take the uncertainty out of politics.

To pick another example, what if there are two candidates for a senatorial nomination, and one is "credentialed" in the sense used in this book (a present or former governor or member of Congress) and the other isn't? And what if, under normal circumstances, the un-credentialed one would win (being better known statewide or whatever), but, because of the keys, the party organization decides to go with the credentialed one, who, therefore, ends up winning the primary? Is the nominee stronger because he's credentialed, or weaker because he's the one who couldn't have won the primary standing on his own?

The closest thing to an answer is that there certainly are times when the less-credentialed candidate should be chosen: the one with credentials is past his prime or tainted by scandal or whatever. Nothing in the keys says these sorts of factors never matter at all, only that they don't directly affect the outcome of elections as often as the eight keys. Figuring out when a credentialed candidate should not be picked over an un-credentialed one would be—as it is today—a matter of judgment.

That ought to please the people who say the keys take the human factor out of politics.

Another "what if": what if a president governs with the keys in mind?

If you were Bill Clinton, and you were elected in 1992, and you knew the keys (as he did), you might well have decided that getting universal health care passed was a ticket to re-election. The accomplishment would turn key 7 (policy change) in your favor. Moreover, it seemed to be the only thing that would. No other issue was ripe.

Of course, Clinton might have pursued the goal even if he didn't have key 7 in mind. All the Democrats in the 1992 presidential primaries were moving toward a universal-coverage plan. So, actually, were many Republicans, because health-insurance costs were soaring and businesses were seeking some sort of overhaul of the system.

In 1994, however, the Republicans were against Clinton's plan; so were some Democrats. And Clinton now appears to have paid a price in the 1994 election for pursuing health care so aggressively, at least in the context of other liberal initiatives. (See Chapter 8.)

So if he was governing with the keys in mind, that backfired.

Perhaps the best advice for a president is to keep the keys in mind but not to stretch too far in an effort to satisfy them. He must keep the times in mind, too. When Clinton came to terms with the times, he thrived and won re-election, even though he gave up on key 7.

As noted earlier, if President George H.W. Bush had had the keys in mind during the Kuwait crisis, he would have done precisely what he did: get in quick, win decisively, get out, and let people gripe, on the one hand, that the war wasn't necessary, or, on the other, that you left Saddam Hussein in power. The foreign-policy-success key was turned.

But Bush didn't have to stretch too far. The opportunity presented itself.

To accompany the above warning to officeholders, here's one for candidates and their supporters:

This book's downplaying of the importance of campaigns should not be interpreted to mean that everybody should take September and October off. As this is written, Lichtman himself is an entry in a senatorial primary. If he gets to the general election, you can bet he will be in high gear, just like other candidates.

The conclusion that campaigns don't determine outcomes is best understood as an answer to a certain question: what happens if both sides try their hardest, which can reasonably be assumed in the kinds of high-stakes races this book is about? The answer is, they cancel each other out. A predictor need only know that they are both in there swinging. For a situation in which only one side is swinging, no guidance is offered in this book.

Suppose you, as a citizen, know that all it will take for your guy to win is for him and his supporters to run as energetic a campaign as the other candidate. And suppose you don't get involved. In that case, given what you now know, you have more to answer to your conscience about than if you think, as many others do, that what determines election outcomes is who has the best media consultant, the more pleasing personality, or the stronger candidates on his side of the ballot in other races.

For those who would hold office, the only clear guidance—the one unavoidable implication—of this book is this: you must find your way into a general election, then get lucky, then govern effectively, as effectiveness is defined by non-partisan, non-ideological people, while you make sure not to give your original supporters cause to turn against you.

Beyond that, the implications of the book for politicians are a matter of judgment. I would say they are liberating.

My advice to candidates would be this: Say what you want to say. It may not help you get elected, but it won't hurt either. If you are in the political mainstream, what you say will find favor with enough people, will not be all that offensive to many others, and will always get you some credit simply for speaking your mind. More people are of the strong opinion that politicians should speak their minds than themselves have strong opinions about any particular controversy that's likely to come up.

In speaking your piece, you will be making your contribution to American political discourse, and you will be setting yourself up to pursue your policy goals if you are elected. You will feel good about your campaign.

If, on the other hand, you are not in the philosophical mainstream, you should probably look for another way to have impact than to hold elective office.

Some people who become familiar with the keys wonder if, as a result of them, fewer mainstream, qualified people will seek office, because they will see more races as hopeless. That would certainly be unfortunate. The nation already has far too many elections that are essentially forfeited by one party or the other, especially when incumbents are on the ballot.

However, the keys shouldn't exacerbate the problem much. As we have seen, they are most powerful with regard to the presidency. In Senate races, while the Lichtman scheme may be more useful than any other in predicting the future, it leaves room for doubt. If there is doubt in the minds of possible challengers who aren't familiar with the keys, familiarity with the keys is unlikely to resolve that doubt, especially given that decisions about running must be made long before the election.

As for the presidency, serious challenges seem likely to continue to occur on schedule. A party has too much too lose by forfeiting the presidency. For one thing, any party wants to force the other one to worry about the presidential race, rather than be able to concentrate all its resources and attention elsewhere. Rightly or wrongly, the party that is hurting in the keys will worry that a presidential landslide or a non-race will hurt it in other races, as well as make it look pathetic to the public and uninterested in national leadership.

Meanwhile, many candidates stand to gain even from a losing challenge to an incumbent president who is seen as unbeatable. Some candidates have always taken passes on particular races. In 1991, President George W. Bush was at stratospheric levels in the polls. This might have played a roll in causing some big names in the party (Bill Bradley, Mario Cuomo,

Sam Nunn) to decide it was the wrong year. But the young governor of Arkansas had nothing to lose.

Anyway, anybody who understands the keys knows they will be wrong some day. And a person who is in the grip of White House fever is more likely than just about anybody to see that day as having arrived.

For—Or About—Campaign Professionals

If the predict-ability of the keys means anything, it is that not many election outcomes have been determined by decisions made about whether to go negative or not, whether to hire a consultant with a national reputation, whether to harp on one issue or another, or whether to make a compromise in pursuit of the financial contributions of one interest group or another.

Let's look at negative campaigning through the prism of Ohio. As this is written, Ohio has two U.S. senators who lost their first bids for that office after running negative campaigns. They won on their second tries, and did so without going negative. Their times simply came.

As noted earlier in the book, George Voinovich ran for the Senate in 1988 against incumbent Democrat and liberal Howard Metzenbaum. Voinovich was one of the great Republican hopes of the year. After hiring a nationally-known, out-of-state media consultant, Voinovich ran a campaign highlighting Metzenbaum's alleged unwillingness to ban child pornography. In other words, he ran a campaign that mirrored the Republican campaign against Democratic presidential nominee Michael Dukakis. But Voinovich never put a dent in the 15-percent lead Metzenbaum started the race with.

Voinovich was elected governor in 1990—the seat was open, being vacated by a Democrat in fairly tough times—and 1994. By 1998, his Senate credentials were as good as they could possibly have been for a person who had never actually been in the Senate. He breezed in overwhelmingly. The only negativity in the campaign was offered by his Democratic opponent, who charged corruption and ran against Voinovich's record as governor; that got the Democrat less than 40 percent of the vote.

Mike DeWine was lieutenant governor under Voinovich. In 1992, he ran against Sen. John Glenn. He ran a thoroughly negative campaign, saying that Glenn may once have been the all-American hero, but had been in Washington too long (18 years) and had been changed by the system. Glenn, after all, had been one of the Keating Five, a group of senators who got in trouble for taking big money from and helping Charles Keating, the financier who eventually went to jail in connection with the savings and loans scandals of the early 1990s. Glenn had been all but exonerated by a Senate investigative committee that was much harsher on three of the other four. But he had also been criticized even by some of his supporters.

The conventional wisdom held that this and other ethics-related problems had rubbed the sheen off Glenn's image, that he was ripe for attack in a year when public hostility toward long-term incumbents was intense. The conventional wisdom also held that there was no way to beat him *but* to go negative. For a while the polls suggested that DeWine's strategy was working, as Glenn's lead disappeared. But Glenn "came back" without doing anything in particular. He won by a seven-point margin that belied even the late polls.

In the end, whatever success DeWine had in bringing Glenn's reputation down to earth was apparently balanced by the price he paid with the voting public for being the guy who set out to do that dirty work to this hero.

Two years later, though, DeWine easily won a Republican primary and breezed through the general election, leaving the negative campaigning to his opponent, who tried to link DeWine with the likes of Jesse Helms.

Neither Voinovich nor DeWine paid any long-term price for demonstrating their willingness to go negative when they were behind against respected figures. A politician has to do a lot more than that to hurt his reputation. But DeWine will always know that he is the guy who went negative against John Glenn, of all people. And when George Voinovich is vaunted publicly—as he often is—for being a cut above the regular politician in decency and in character and in concern for substance, an embarrassing memory may always nag at him about the Metzenbaum race.

In the three months before the 1998 congressional elections, the phrase "going negative works" or "negative campaigning works" or "negative campaigns work" appeared in newspapers in New York, Los Angeles, London, Cleveland, Boston, Atlanta, Fort Worth, Phoenix, Jacksonville, Palm Beach, Sarasota, Topeka, Orange County (Cal.), Columbus (Oh.),

Salt Lake City, Orlando, and Charleston (W. Va.). These were in separate articles, not wire stories run simultaneously by many papers.

However, my own sense—hard to document—is that the belief that negative campaigns work was all but universal in the political world in the early 1990s, and that by 1998 a view had started to set in that there is sometimes a price to pay.

And if we are going to wonder about negative campaigning, we should wonder about the high-priced consultants who often bring it to us. We should wonder whether they know anything about politics that is worth knowing and isn't merely common sense. We should wonder whether a candidate really needs anybody advising him on politics at any level beyond "make sure your zippers are zipped and your hair is combed."

I doubt it. I suspect that if you just hire somebody who knows the mechanics of putting a fund-raiser together, knows how to get a commercial produced and on the air, and who makes sure that you are scheduled for a lot of campaign events, that's enough. As to the matter of how to campaign, you can follow your own instincts. A smart candidate needs an aide, not a consultant or adviser.

Some candidates have limited their intake of money and won re-elections: Sens. William Proxmire and Russ Feingold in Wisconsin; Sen. and Gov. Lawton Chiles in Florida. It's not that big a leap to limiting one's intake of professional advice.

For Journalists

The journalists—especially the young ones—are the audience I am most interested in. However dismissive this book might sound at times about my chosen field, I know that most news people want to tell the story as it really is, and I know that if they are getting it wrong, that's because strong forces are driving them astray.

When I was in graduate school, I was exposed to a book called *The Structure of Scientific Revolutions*, by Thomas Kuhn. I say "was exposed to" rather than "read," because I simply could not read it; it was too hard. What I know about it, I heard in seminars. I have always remembered one point: Kuhn says that the way scientific revolutions happen—the acceptance of Newton's theories, say, or Einstein's or Darwin's—is not that a scientist publishes a paper, and all the other scientists read it and offer a joint "Eureka!"

What happens is that most of the other leading scientists remain skeptical but eventually retire and are replaced by a younger generation that does accept the new idea.

(If that isn't a good reading of Kuhn, blame the people in my seminar. I recently bought the book again for purposes of writing this book, but I still can't read it.)

The Kuhn process is the one I have in mind for change in the way people think about American politics. Until the older generation gives way, the progress can only be incremental.

Some progress has happened. As suggested elsewhere in this book, politicos and journalists alike have given various indications of having been influenced by Lichtmanesque ideas. But there has been no collective "Eureka!"

The articles that have been written about the keys—by now quite a few—have been basically positive; indeed, the keys have gotten almost no critical treatment, either in academic or journalistic publications. But the attention has been brief, sporadic and almost a running sideshow to what I guess Kuhn would call the prevailing "paradigm": the obsession with image manipulation.

Another reason I think the triumph of correct analysis will be gradual is that I only came to believe in the keys gradually myself. First, after being exposed to them, I was intrigued, but skeptical. I kept them in mind through a couple of election cycles, then became a believer. I expect that to be the pattern for others. I suppose we all believe in learning the way we learned.

Anyway, I've been writing opinion pieces about a lot of subjects for 20-some years, and I have learned this: Nobody ever changes anybody else's mind. People change their own minds occasionally. (In politics, the number of such occasions annually in a mid-size state can probably be counted on one hand). But they do so at their own pace, for their own inscrutable reasons.

Suppose, however, that some journalists do eventually decide that Lichtman is fundamentally right. What then? What's the best way to do campaign coverage, consistent with that view?

To argue that campaigns don't determine election outcomes is not to argue that campaigns are unimportant. A campaign gets the politicians on record on the issues. It validates the notion that what democracy is all about is the consent of the governed. It generates a kind of feedback from the public that the politicians notice. It informs citizens about what's going on (if not all people, then enough to matter). It gives people their chance to join in.

And even if campaigns don't result in clear decisions about competing mainstream views, they do help in defining what's in the mainstream and what isn't, what goes and what doesn't. Much gets weeded out in the course of a long campaign year.

The fundamental way for journalists to deal with the important events playing out in campaigns is simply to report what the candidates say (and don't say), and how the message is received, and how it changes through a campaign. Reporters and their editors should not be too leery of repetition. What's old to journalists by the fall is new to most people. Summarizing long speeches remains a service throughout the campaign, perhaps being even more valuable at the end, when people are really focused.

Reporters should ask more questions about policy, including the candidate's record on it, and fewer about politics.

I would not put any ban on "horse-race" stuff, that is, the news about campaign tactics and strategies, about the polls, about the size of a candidate's budget, about what's happening on the Internet, and about the hiring and firing of campaign consultants. I might relegate it to an inside page, or a Sunday column with a collection of two-and-three-paragraph mini-stories. But it's legitimate fodder. Just as Hollywood reporters tell us about what's going on behind the scenes, just as sports reporters go into the locker rooms, political reporters should tell us more about a campaign than is immediately visible.

They just shouldn't take the inside stuff seriously. The strongest case against the "horse-race" coverage is that it is wrong-headed. Elections are simply not much like horse races. The win will often not go to the swiftest. Swiftness hardly even counts in general elections; or, at least, the differences in swiftness that are present are generally too small to count, because a really slow horse is not likely to make it to the gate. To try to find an important difference between the campaigns is to engage in hair splitting; and differences so small don't make a difference.

Once that is understood, fine, let's hear the inside stuff.

I would put a ban on questions about how a candidate expects to win, given this political problem or that one. I'd make a follow-up question along such lines punishable by imprisonment. Let the candidate worry about how to win.

I would not spend much time asking how a candidate expects to mollify this or that critic in the party, or expects to bring a defeated rival on board. If the candidate wants to bring that up, fine. But the fundamental issue for journalists ought to be how he or she plans to govern the nation, not win the election.

I would not ask a candidate to explain a bad poll. This sort of question is strange work, after all; when we are not complaining about the politicians "spinning" us, we are inviting them to.

Perhaps my overarching rule would be this: let's come to terms with the fact that we political journalists prefer politics to policy. The process and personalities and competition are what fascinate us. So we are too eager to believe they are what's important. We need to work hard to stay open to the possibility that they are not.

In deciding how to cover campaigns, we need to recognize that something is wrong in the American political system. The problem manifests itself not only in often-low voter turnout, but in a certain sourness about the workings of democracy, even when things are going relatively well for the nation.

The job of journalists isn't to promote democracy any more than they do, but to make sure they get the story of democracy right. To keep leaving people with the impression that image manipulation and money are everything in politics would be necessary if it were true. But it's not true, and the misimpression can't be doing any good.

For Democracy

Some might suggest that the keys leave as much room for cynicism about democracy as does conventional analysis. After all, presidents and candidates get no credit in the keys for thinking brilliantly and bravely about the nation's long-term problems. The presidential keys are all about the short-term.

The Senate keys aren't about policy issues at all.

And nothing in either set of keys deals with any sort of moral imperative along the lines of comforting the afflicted or promoting good "family values."

But this is all because the keys boil down to a contemplation of the concerns of swing voters. These voters don't seem to see aligning with a party as a way of promoting their long-term or moral concerns.

Where long-term and moral concerns come into play regularly is through the votes of the partisans.

In 1980, by the standards of the keys, Jimmy Carter was the virtual definition of an ineffective president; he lost eight keys. But, still, 42 percent of the voters supported him. These are people who don't ask questions about whether a president is effective in foreign policy, or about how the economy is doing. They vote on what a person stands for (as indicated by party label). They implicitly believe or even explicitly insist that if the country's leadership has the right values, then the country will benefit in the long run, even if it isn't doing so well now under that leadership.

The long-term and moral concerns of the two parties determine a lot about how the nation is governed. The Republican interest in limiting governmental intrusion in economic matters is a big part of the explanation for this society's economic system being more vibrantly capitalistic than that of some other democracies. The Democrats' long-term interest in limiting government intrusion into private lives and in tending to the interests of the poor and the struggling have achieved and sustained such long-term policies as legal abortion, Social Security and Medicare.

The voters who choose which set of values they want to promote in the long term are having impact. The fact that neither party ever succeeds in stamping out the other doesn't change that.

A system in which people with long-term concerns shape the parties, and people with short-term concerns shape the party make-up of the government, has a certain logic.

When I became interested in the Lichtman system, it wasn't because

I thought the prevailing understanding of American democracy was harmful. I just wanted to understand things better.

But the Lichtman system turns out to have more than understanding to offer. It offers a view of democracy that sustains belief in democracy. If adopted in any widespread way, it offers the prospect of a time when journalists present a picture of democracy that is not so irritating and childish; when candidates and politicians worry less about images and more about substantive contributions, and when the American people see politics as a more respectable and meaningful exercise.

Like so much that comes from the purveyors of the conventional understanding of American politics, the initial widespread reaction to the Lichtman system is wrong. This stuff is not bad news. It's good news.

CHAPTER

14

2008: Race Never an Issue

Not long before writing this chapter in late 2016, I was talking with an old Jewish friend about the possibility of a Jew being elected president in our time. He thought it couldn't happen. This caused me to think that already some people had forgotten just how unlikely the election of a Barack Obama would have seemed a few years before it happened. To document how unlikely it seemed is a little bit difficult, because the possibility was seldom discussed publicly. But this much is fair to say:

If in, say, 2003, you had raised the question "Can a black man be elected president of the United States in our time?" you could have generated a debate. Some people certainly would have granted the possibility, most likely under carefully described circumstances. But if you then specified that by "our time," you meant 2008, you would have sharply reduced the number of, shall we say, optimists. If you then specified that you had in mind a liberal Democrat, the number would have shrunk further; many people thought the first black president would have to be a Republican war hero or something like that, a person whose persona was peculiarly soothing to people who might be skeptical. The name of Colin Powell would have come up. He was the very popular retired black general who was secretary of state 2003. He had been discussed as a possible presidential candidate, and few people had laughed. (However his wife was widely reported to have nixed the idea, because she thought a black president would be particularly likely to be assassinated. Nobody could laugh at that, either.)

But if you specified that you wanted to discuss the possible election of a person who had no great resume in politics, the military, sports or anything else, but was a merely junior senator whose pre-political career had been as a community organizer, you would have been accused of stacking the deck in favor of a negative response. If you then had specified the guy's name would be Barack Obama, you would have been accused of insulting the intelligence of those engaged. And if you gave him the middle-name Hussein, you would have been accused of turning the whole thing into a joke.

In 2004, the discussion changed somewhat, because Obama – theretofore unheard of – made a big splash as the keynote speaker at the Democratic National Convention when he decried political polarization – blue states and red states and all that. His name came up as a presidential contender for the future. People couldn't ignore his success in Illinois in that year. (He was overwhelmingly elected to the U.S. Senate. It so happened that his opponent was black, too, but that candidate was a late substitute after the expected Republican candidacy collapsed. Everybody granted that the Republicans simply didn't have anybody who could beat Obama.)

Still, as 2008 approached, the race thing and the name thing were discussed endlessly. The year 2008 was widely seen as too soon. And Hillary Clinton was generally seen as having a lock on the nomination. In 2009, the liberal blog *The Daily Kos* collected a bunch of predictions made in the run-up to 2008. A partial list:

Oct. 27, 2006: "[Obama] should run in '08. He will lose in '08. And the loss will put him irrevocably on a path to the presidency." For him to win in '08 would require a "miracle." – Charles Krauthammer, conservative commentator.

Dec. 17, 2006: "Barack Obama is not going to beat Hillary Clinton in a single Democratic primary. I'll predict that right now." – William Kristol, conservative commentator.

Dec. 22, 2006: "Obama's shot at the top will be short lived.... Hillary Inc. will grind up and spit out any Democratic challenger that gets in its way." – Joe Scarborough, Republican commentator.

Mar. 19, 2007: "The right knows Obama is unelectable except perhaps against Attila the Hun." – Mark Penn, Hillary Clinton aide.

Sep. 24, 2007: "Sen. Obama cannot possibly believe, and doesn't even act as if he believes, that he can be elected president of the United States next year." – Christopher Hitchens, leftish but unpredictable commentator.

Jan. 26, 2008: "The 'could we beat Obama?' conversation is purely academic. It's over. The Clintons have defeated him already, because he is leaving South Carolina as 'the black candidate.' He won't win another state." – Michael Graham, *National Review*, conservative magazine.

May 7, 2008: "[Obama] has shown he cannot get the votes Democrats need to win – blue-collar, working class people. He can get effete snobs, he can get wealthy academics, he can get the young, and he can get the black vote, but Democrats do not win with that.... He will lose big." – Rush Limbaugh, conservative commentator.

June 3, 2008: "Obama can't possibly be elected." – Dick Morris, Democratic and Republican operative turned Republican commentator.

The Daily Kos also took note that In 2007, Shelby Steele, a prominent conservative black intellectual who focused on racial matters, wrote a book called *"A Bound Man: Why We Are Excited about Obama and Why He Can't Win."* Steele wasn't arguing that voters were too racist, but that race was a complicated, sensitive subject that left Obama conflicted and that he hadn't sufficiently figured out how to handle. Steele was coming very close to saying race was still too dicey.

Tom Hayden, famed left-wing, then liberal activist said on Sept. 25 of the election year: "An African-American candidate talking about economics and a white war hero – it's clear to me who is going to win." (Reported in the *Huffington Post* on that date.)

The issue – was everywhere. The online publication *Slate* ran a piece in January subtitled "What the claims that a black man is unelectable say about the rest of us."

But Lichtman predicted the Democrats' victory in November before anybody knew whether their candidate would be a black man – and he never waffled later, much less changed his prediction. He made it March of 2007, in a column in the Gazette newspapers in suburban Maryland, outside Washington.

Then, in a piece appearing on the *History News Network* site in early October, 2007, he put it this way: "The Democrats will recapture the White House next fall, whether they nominate Hillary Rodham Clinton or

Barack Obama, John Edwards, or Bill Richardson. Only an unprecedented cataclysmic change in American politics during the next year could salvage Republican hopes."

In other words: white woman, black man, white man or white man of mainly Mexican descent (Richardson). Whatever.

By Lichtman's count, seven keys could already be turned against the Republicans in 2007, one more than was necessary to predict a Democratic victory. The 2006 midterm election had been horrible for the Republicans, with Democrats taking over both the House and Senate. The pending and presumably hot race for the Republican nomination would cost that party a key. The fact that the incumbent president wasn't on the ballot was a problem. So was George W. Bush's lack of a major new policy achievement in his second term.

Then there was Iraq. Although the U.S. "surge" in Iraq in early 2007 was widely deemed a success at the time in reducing levels of violence and stabilizing the country, Lichtman called the foreign policy failure key against the Republicans, because the U.S. was still bogged down there. After all, nobody in this country would have defined success in the Iraq war as a reduction in violence to levels prevailing earlier in the war. Meanwhile, there was no countervailing success elsewhere, and the foreign policy success key fell.

Finally, the Republicans seemed unlikely to nominate a charismatic person or a national hero for president. Of course, John McCain, the ultimate nominee, is referred to in the vernacular as a "national hero" because of his heroic behavior as a long-term prisoner of war. In denying him the label, Lichtman was certainly not agreeing with Donald Trump's later denigration of McCain's service. Lichtman was just using the term "national hero" differently. As noted in earlier chapters, just having an admirable military record doesn't win the key. John Kennedy's World War II heroism was a universally known fact in 1960, but it didn't get him the key. John Kerry's medal-winning war record would not have won him the key even if the Republicans had not disputed his record. What Lichtman meant by "national hero" was somebody like Dwight Eisenhower or Ulysses S. Grant, men with whom the entire country had gone through a long crisis.

So the Democrats got the overall call even without counting Barack

Obama's charisma or the massive recession that began in 2008. Lichtman didn't turn those keys until later, when because of the recession, he also turned the long-term economy key against the Republicans.

To underline that last point: Those who think elections are all about the economy might note that Lichtman made his call without calling either economy key. And those who argue – as some did after the election – that it was, in fact, the collapse of the economy in late 2008 that defeated McCain, again it is worth noting that Lichtman made his prediction without knowing that was coming and, in effect, without caring whether it did or not.

The only keys he gave the Republicans in 2007 were for the absence of a major scandal and major social unrest, and the presumed absence of charisma in the Democratic nominee, on which he later changed his mind.

He also changed on another key, which would have mattered a lot more if the overall key count had been close. Early in 2007, he assumed the Republican nomination would be hotly contested, costing the Republicans a key. Then he concluded that it hadn't been. McCain wrapped up the nomination in the spring, and the August convention was united behind him.

In the year before the election, the polls generally favored Obama over McCain (judging by the *Real Clear Politics* average of polls), but almost never by as much as Obama's 7.2 percent victory margin. McCain had leads in December and January, then again in March and May and September, but narrowly. Through it all, many commentators were all but certain that there would be a "Bradley effect" at work. This was a reference to black candidate Tom Bradley's loss for mayor of Los Angeles in 1982 after he led in the polls. Many people believed that an anti-black vote materialized only in the voting booth, not in opinion polls, because poll respondents didn't want to be seen as racists. But, in the end, Obama actually outperformed his late-poll average.

Lichtman certainly was not alone in seeing a Democratic victory, particularly given the polls. But he was remarkably – as far as I know, uniquely – early and remarkably certain, especially given the race factor.

The point of Lichtman's discounting of race was never that we had reached some post-racial phase of American politics. Race was still a huge factor in American political life. It shaped our political parties. Civil rights issues had driven blacks to the Democratic Party. Hard-core racists and others who found the resulting Democratic Party too liberal had long since taken note and left the party. In 2008, they would have voted against Hillary Clinton, too.

Of course, that still left the possibility of other white people voting based on race, the way ethnic groups have often voted for one of their own. Surely that still happens. But the people who thought Obama would be weak in a general election don't get the different roles played by primaries and generals. The nomination process is where historic changes in public attitudes on race or other demographic characteristics of the candidates – and even on ideology – are likely to be tested. Could a Catholic be elected in 1960? Could a Southerner win in 1976 (without being the incumbent, as Lyndon Johnson was in 1964)? Could somebody as conservative as Ronald Reagan prevail? These were all hotly contested questions.

The answer is pretty clear: If a candidate can show enough skill and appeal to win a major-party nomination, then he or she can win the election, depending on which party has a leg up in that year. The demographic or ideological label in question could be expected to lose the candidate some support and win some. But that would play out in the primaries. In the general election, party labels and the change issue come to the fore.

When Obama beat Hillary, that's when we knew that times had changed enough for a black man – indeed, a liberal, inexperienced black man named Barack Hussein Obama – to be elected president.

CHAPTER

15

2012: Obamacare an Asset?
Lichtman vs. Silver

In middle and late 2011, things did not look great for Barack Obama. The nation's recovery from the extraordinary recession he inherited was painfully slow. His party had suffered a huge rejection in the mid-term election of 2010, losing 63 seats in the House of Representatives and control of that body. This came after the birth of the Tea Party movement, a highly spirited rebellion against "big government" under both Obama and his predecessor George W. Bush. All the political energy seemed to be on the right. After bitter, scary negotiations in Washington about raising and paying the federal debt, Obama's public approval dipped as low as 38 percent in the third quarter of 2011 and generally hovered in the low 40s in the last half of the year, according to Gallup.

But when, on June 17, 2011, I wrote a Lichtman-channeling column in the *Dayton Daily News*, I was able to begin it like this:

"Obama.

"You were wondering who wins the 2012 election, right? And, based on experience, you came here, right? Well, it's Obama."

In calling the keys, Lichtman was giving Obama credit for bringing major change with Obamacare and with his huge stimulus package to combat the recession he inherited. Lichtman was also giving Obama credit for a major foreign policy victory: the killing of Osama bin Laden, the mastermind of the 9/11 attacks.

Beyond that, he was assuming that Obama would not only be the nominee but would breeze to re-nomination (two keys); that there would be no major scandal, social unrest or foreign policy failure, and that the Republicans would not have a charismatic candidate.

Meanwhile, he was awarding the Republicans only three keys: they had more seats in the House than before 2008; Obama's charisma had worn off (a very close call, said Lichtman); and the long-term economy would help the Republicans, because the effects of the recession were felt mainly on Obama's watch.

Lichtman left two keys uncalled: the short-term economy (recession in the election year) and whether there'd be a significant third party, though he said probably not.

He saw no realistic way for the Republicans to get to six.

Some of Lichtman's calls might be disputed and need to be paused over, specifically those involving Obamacare, bin Laden and Obama's alleged lack of charisma.

Obamacare: Lichtman actually said on March 26, 2010 (!) that "Enactment of the health care reform bill nearly guarantees President Barack Obama's re-election in 2012."

The notion of Obamacare as a political asset to the president was shocking to the conventional wisdom. The health care reform law did a lot. Most importantly, it was an effort to dramatically decrease the number of people (then 30 million) who had no health insurance. It approached that goal by requiring most people who didn't have health insurance through their jobs to purchase it and by subsidizing those who couldn't afford it. The law was passed on a partisan vote. It was playing badly in 2011, as before and after. Polls typically showed about half the population opposing it and maybe 40 percent in support (see, for example, the fact-checking site *Politifact* in February 2011). Of course, some people who opposed the law thought it didn't go far enough. Yet all the political energy, all the intense emotion seemed to be with the anti-big government opponents. The Republicans had ridden the issue in 2010 and, as a result of their victories, were more emboldened than ever against it. Just about any conventional political analyst would have told you in 2011 that Obamacare would be a problem for the Democrats in 2012, not an asset.

One example is Nate Silver, of the *FiveThirtyEight* website. In a lengthy, multi-pronged critique of the prediction (considered further below), he noted that both Obamacare and the stimulus package "are rather unpopular." He asked, "On what premise will they increase (Obama's) re-election chances?"

The premise is explained at length and explicitly in Lichtman's original book on the keys, *"The Thirteen Keys to the Presidency,"* (Ken DeCell co-author) from 1990 (pages 81 and 82):

"The electorate clearly rewards dynamism and change. The executive party has won fourteen of seventeen elections when it has effected major changes in national policy during the term (win rate: 82 percent), and it has lost ten of the sixteen in which it has been content with the status quo (loss rate: 62 percent).... Implementing broad new initiatives gives the executive party an image of accomplishment and success, and the changes enacted usually address widely perceived needs. Moreover, the ability to push through controversial new measures – and major changes in national policy are almost always controversial – reflects both the underlying strength and the political skills of a president and his party."

Despite all that, admittedly, it would not be beyond reason to suggest that Obamacare might be the exception. But Obamacare combined with the Obama stimulus and the bailout of the auto industry made quite a record of change. There certainly was a rationale for Lichtman's case.

Few political analysts in the media consider the possibility that an issue can play one way (against the Democrats, say) in a mid-term and the opposite way in a presidential election.

In Obama in 2010, nonpartisan voters saw a president who had enacted a lot of hugely important stuff without any support from the opposing party. In fact, he had made that party apoplectic about him and about what was happening to the country. These nonpartisan voters had to decide in 2010 whether they wanted more of that. If they wanted to see the values of both parties reflected in policy, their likely vote was for Republicans in the mid-term to achieve balance.

But in a presidential election, the question for voters is not whether both parties' views should be reflected, but who should be president. In 2012, one argument that could not be made against Obama was weakness. Obamacare was one reason he had emerged as a genuine leader.

Nonpartisan voters seem to want that in a president, even if they aren't convinced he is totally right about policy.

Osama bin Laden: Before 2011, Lichtman said that getting bin Laden would get Obama a key, because "the capture or killing of bin Laden has been a major objective of American foreign policy for nearly a decade. And presidents who achieve major American objectives typically win election."

Bin Laden was killed on May 2, 2011. Obama's approval ratings in polls jumped 8-10 points. By June, however, Obama was already losing the "bump." The political media – partisan and non-partisan alike – were fascinated by that.

Radio provocateur Rush Limbaugh is particularly fun to quote. On June 8, he reprised a clip of him talking a few weeks earlier:

"Killing Osama is not gonna change one thing about why people are upset with Obama. And I'm telling you, there's gonna be an uptick (that is, the bump) in the polls. Get ready for that this week. But it's going to pass."

Then he went live: "It's going to pass. And, my friends, it has passed. State-controlled media is scratching their heads. They had Obama reelected. They want to know – we have a montage here – what happened to the Bin Laden bounce."

Here Limbaugh presented audio clips of 10 people, including commentators Karl Rove, Bill O'Reilly, and Mika Brzezinski and foreign Democratic cabinet member Janet Napolitano, noting that the bump had vanished or was vanishing.

Said one: "Any laurels (Obama) might have rested upon following the death of bin Laden have certainly been pulled from under his feet."

Back to Limbaugh:

"It's gone. Gone. But you didn't need to wait for the montage today to know because I, El Rushbo, told you it wouldn't last. And anybody with any common sense would have been able to tell you this."

But to win re-election, Obama did not need the polls in the spring of 2011 to reflect his success in this grizzly matter. He needed the public reacting in a certain way in November of 2012, after all the events of the previous four years had been sifted. The polls of 2011 didn't tell you which events would matter and which wouldn't. Systematic contemplation of historical patterns told you that.

Obama's Charisma: Lichtman had always struggled with this subject.

In 2008, he had been slow in turning the key for the Democrats. Now he was worried that Obama's fragile charisma – which had certainly been fostered in some degree by his newness on the scene – had been a casualty of the recurring ugly, hyper-partisan battles of the Obama era.

I always had a problem explaining to friends at the newspaper and elsewhere how anyone might not consider Obama charismatic. To them, Obama's charisma was a given. I tried to explain that Lichtman's standard was very high, that Bill Clinton didn't qualify. There's got be some sort of trans-party appeal, a sense of a special force at work, something that is entirely about personality, not issues.

But I think the point I should fall back on is one noted earlier in this book: that Lichtman has designed his system to allow for rare differences of opinion on calling the keys. Specifically, he tries to make sure that no prediction depends on any one key. He achieved that in both Obama elections. Moreover, as he points out, no election has ever been called as the result of a charisma key being turned for a candidate.

I don't want to pretend that in 2011 everybody but Lichtman thought Obama was going to lose. What I said in my June column – trying to capture the political atmosphere at the time – was "Everyplace you turn these days, the pundits are saying the 2012 election is up for grabs and that the outcome depends on the economy and how successfully the contending parties spin it." That conventional wisdom was wrong in every regard. The economy would not be decisive – and that was knowable in 2011.

Fast-forwarding to after that election, we find the usual half-baked, self-serving explanations for its outcome. In Nov. 2012, Steve Forbes, a former presidential candidate, wrote in *Forbes* magazine about "The Five Reasons Romney Lost." The first was "The Napoleon Factor," meaning Obama was a lucky guy. (Napoleon said he would prefer a lucky general to a good one.) Said Forbes, "In 2008, the Democratic challenger was slightly behind McCain after Labor Day. Then came the financial panic, which helped him win. This time (2012), (Hurricane) Sandy hit the Northeast; the President suddenly took on the Olympian mantle of crisis leadership, aided immensely by hugs from the New Jersey GOP Governor. Romney's momentum was stopped cold."

Two: "Obama Dominated the Ground Game." Three: "Romney Allowed the Other Side to Define Him & GOP Agenda." You get the idea.

Forbes didn't go to a frequent canard about the campaign: that Mitt Romney's fateful mistake was saying in May of 2012 that 47 percent of the voters were out of his reach because they didn't pay federal income taxes and were, in fact, dependent on the government, and were, therefore, natural Democrats. Surely that was a blunder by Romney; it caused him embarrassment. But Obama blew the first debate. The blunders washed out – as usual.

Forbes wasn't entirely alone in his analysis. In January of 2016, Romney's political strategist Stuart Stevens told the *Huffington Post* that the 2012 hurricane was a big political problem. Said *HuffPo* in paraphrasing Stevens, "A president who was looking for a message suddenly was being praised for his poise and leadership." Said Stevens, "It definitely cost us Florida. I think it definitely cost us Virginia. I can't tell you if it cost Ohio. I can't tell you it cost us Colorado."

But in 2011, Lichtman did not predict an October-surprise hurricane in 2012. He talked only about what had already happened by mid-2011.

In every election, it seems, a new circumstance arises that causes some people who are confronted with the long-term success of the keys to suspect that this is the year when the keys will go awry. In 2008, obviously, it was race (or, during the primaries, gender). I found in conversations about 2012 with various journalists and other politicos that the new circumstance on many minds was the Supreme Court decision known as Citizens United. In that decision, the court had invalidated restraints on the size of corporate contributions to committees advocating for – and buying television ads for – candidates. Some people believed this great unleashing of the corporations represented a sea change in American politics.

Those people weren't much interested in hearing about a predictive system that had proven successful in another historical era, i.e., before 2010. They were victims of the conventional fascination with money, media manipulation and television ads in politics. In fact, however, few things in the world matter less than commercials in a presidential election.

As Lichtman has said, "The people who vote know who you are and what you stand for. You don't need paid media." Citizens United was a non-issue.

———

Let's circle back to Nate Silver. In Chapter 3, we considered some of the other predictive systems extant when Lichtman started making his predictions in the 1980s. In this century, however, a new fellow emerged unmistakably as the national predictor in chief: At first as a regular feature in *The New York Times*, Silver made a big splash in 2008, predicting Obama's win and being overwhelmingly right about specific states and specific Senate races. He made his predictions in terms of probabilities: There's X percent chance something will happen. And he changed the percentages as events and polls unfold. When people talked about him being "right," they were often referring to predictions made near the end of the campaign.

Silver was widely read and quoted. Familiarity with his latest pronouncements was the sign of the true politico, even of the well-read citizen with a taste for numbers. He was seen as the guy who got beyond the headlines of the day and dealt with more meaningful matters. His reputation seemed to benefit from not being a journalist, far more than Lichtman's ever had.

But, conversely, he also seemed to benefit from the fact that, like a journalist, he was always coming out with new stuff: new numbers, new polls, new poll analyses, new probabilities. People followed him throughout a campaign in a way that couldn't happen in the case of a predictor who simply stated an outcome and stuck with it – and who didn't have a great national outlet.

I won't speak for Lichtman, but Silver's rise was frustrating for me. I saw what he was doing as not remotely as impressive as what Lichtman was doing, nor as interesting (lacking the new insights about what does and does not drive election outcomes). He also did not have Lichtman's long track record.

Lichtman's flat prediction about 2012 came to Silver's attention in the summer of 2011. You can imagine how a predictor – Silver – who was just gearing up for 2012 might have felt about a predictor who said all the important factors dictating the 2012 outcome had already happened.

Silver devoted his blog on August 31, 2011, to Lichtman. His headline: "Despite Keys, Obama Is No Lock." He started with a critique of the subjectivity of the keys. That's where everybody starts, and it can be done in a way that's fair enough. (Of course, by then Lichtman had a public record for being right many times in a row – with the arguable exception of 1992 – and often very early. One might think that would obviate at least some of the concern about subjectivity. But OK.)

Then Silver simply went astray. He said, for example that, "It's less that (Lichtman) has discovered the right set of keys than that he's a locksmith and can keep minting new keys until he happens to open all 38 doors." This referred to the number of consecutive elections Lichtman said the keys call, most of them retroactively.

But, of course, Lichtman does not keep minting new keys. He uses the same ones all the time. Even if he kept inventing new ones, the fact that he was predicting accurately so early – as in the case of 2012 – would have to be confronted. But the fact he doesn't mint new keys is central to the whole enterprise.

In suggesting that Lichtman might select his keys artfully, Silver said "one can conceivably think of any number of other areas that might have been included in the formula but which are not — looking at how messy the primaries were for the opposition party, for example, or the inflation rate, or the ideological positioning of the candidates. (I mention these particular ones because there is some empirical evidence that they do matter.)"

It is apparent that Silver hadn't read Lichtman's book, perhaps because he didn't know there was a book. He seemed to be writing off a column.

He gives no indication of familiarity with Lichtman's explanation for the development of the keys. To wit – as explained in Lichtman's book – he and his colleagues started with the premise that victory or defeat for incumbent parties had something to do with how things had gone on their watch. The idea was that voters were pragmatic and were judging performance. The researchers tested some possible variables they could think of, along these performance-based lines and other lines. They asked how these variables had played out in past elections.

From Lichtman's book: "The initial list of variables comprised some thirty questions dealing with domestic and foreign-policy issues, candidate and party ideology, the unity and strength of the major parties, past election results, whether the nation was a war or peace, economic performance, policy change, social unrest, presidential scandal, campaign finance, candidates' personality traits, third-party activities, vice-presidential nominations, campaign strategy, and the number of consecutive terms the incumbent party had been in office."

Other researchers starting with other predispositions might have tested other variables. But final selection of the keys wasn't arbitrary. It wasn't off the top of the head. At any rate, only some of those tested turned out to be highly correlated with victory.

Turning specifically to the 2012 prediction, Silver said, "As for Mr. Obama, I'd note that only two of Mr. Lichtman's 13 keys pertain to the economy, or 15 percent (of the keys). Even our Republican readers, I think, would be ready to concede him another four years if the economy accounted for only 15 percent of voters' decision.... But chances are that the economy is going to be much more important than that: my research suggest that it accounts for about half of a voter's decision."

Silver isn't getting it. The economy can affect other keys, too: the midterm election outcome; whether the incumbent party is united; whether a substantial third party develops; the social-unrest key. If the economy is somewhere in the normal range, it's not likely to have big effects on other keys; other factors are likely to be more important in determining the outcome of the election.

After dealing with Obamacare issue (as noted above), Silver focuses on the fact that there's no big correlation between the number of keys a winner is accorded and the size of his eventual victory. He sees this as meaningful, on the premise that if you can't predict margin, but you're nevertheless predicting winners, you're just getting lucky on winners. You're riding for a fall.

Silver allowed Lichtman a long rebuttal, which ran on Sept. 12, 2011. Lichtman attempted to minimize the extent to which vote margins differed from key margins. I was surprised that he took up the issue at all, because I had never seen his system as being about margins, just victories. I think that Lichtman had gradually become more concerned about this particular issue because it was raised by other academics. The fact, for example, that the 1960 election was a squeaker though the keys pointed overwhelmingly to a Kennedy victory certainly suggests a vulnerability in the system. But in the early days Lichtman had said the main purpose of having as many as 13 keys – which can result in a wide margin in the keys – was not to get a feel for the impending vote margin, but to increase the probability of an accurate victory prediction.

Concluding, Silver said, "In short, be suspicious of results that seem too good to be true. I'm probably in a minority here, but if two interns applied to 538, and one of them claimed to have a formula that predicted 33 of 38 elections correctly, and the other one said that they had got all 38 right, I'd hire the first one without giving it a second thought – it's far more likely that she understood the limitations of empirical and statistical analysis."

But Lichtman wasn't an intern. He had the skills and resources and time to nail this and an academic reputation to worry about.

Anyway, you don't have to accept Lichtman's claim to be able to retroactively "predict" the outcomes of the elections before 1984 (that is, the 38). His claim is subject to legitimate skepticism on grounds of the subjectivity of some keys, plus the fact that most of us simply don't know enough history to argue with Lichtman about his calls. No matter. Now we have the post-1984 record. Lichtman made his calls publicly. And he made them flatly (that is, with none of Silver's beloved percentages).

After talking about "minting" new keys, Silver says, "These types of problems, which are technically known as overfitting and data dredging, are among the most important things you ought to learn about in a well-taught econometrics class – but many published economists and political scientists seem to ignore them when it comes to elections forecasting."

A serious charge of corner-cutting – at best – from a guy who hadn't done the reading but reached conclusions anyway. By the time Silver critiqued him, Lichtman had been around for decades, appearing in scholarly journals and at national conferences of scholars. It's interesting that Silver didn't know what was going on in the field of scholarly political predictions. He didn't invent it.

Lichtman's early prediction notwithstanding, I cannot report that Lichtman himself was always absolutely certain about 2012. After Obama's bad performance in the first debate with Romney – when the polls were close – Lichtman was appalled and nervous. He said the logic of the keys assumes a certain minimal competence on both sides. As I've noted, he has always said that the keys will fail one day; he has not insisted that he can predict what circumstances might cause that. So he watches events with uncertainty, too.

CHAPTER

16

2016: A Celebrated Mistake

In 2016, the keys failed. Very narrowly, they predicted a victory by Donald Trump. They have always been presented as predicting the popular vote, which wasn't even very close in going for Hillary Clinton.

Ironically, though, in the wake of the election, Lichtman was featured and celebrated in the media – including the elite media – as never before. He was hot. Finally.

The *Washington Post's* Chris Cillizza wrote on New Year's Eve 2016 that his columns about Lichtman had attracted more readers to *The Fix* (which Cillizza jointly operated) that year than anything.

"(E)very time Lichtman said, well, anything, readers flocked. Of the 10 most trafficked posts on *The Fix* in 2016, four involved Lichtman and his unorthodox predictions," he said. "Those four posts totaled more than 10 million unique visitors alone and were four of the 37 most trafficked posts on the entire *(Washington Post)* website this year. 2016 was most definitely the Year of Lichtman."

The interest started when Lichtman made his call in late September. The headlines read simply that he predicted a Trump victory; they made no distinction between the popular and electoral votes. Whichever vote tally you were talking about, however, to say that this prediction cut dramatically against the grain is to make a point that needs no documenting, at least to contemporary readers (presumably the only ones).

But, OK, one piece of documentation. We're talking about a campaign in which leading Democratic campaign operative James Carville sent out a letter in mid-October saying the Trump campaign was "dunzo" ("It launched. It failed miserably. It died.") The point of the letter was that contributors should send their money to congressional candidates, because the only question now was whether the Democrats would win "the whole enchilada."

When Lichtman made his call, some people were shocked, in the most negative sense. Some were thrilled. Just about any politico who came across the prediction had to be struck.

The prediction was covered by the *New York Times*, the *Post*, *NPR*, and *Reuters*, and it was in newspapers around the country via various wires. Over the remainder of the campaign, reporters would double back to Lichtman to see if he was sticking with his call (after certain news events that seemed utterly devastating to Trump and will be noted below). He was, but nervously.

On the day after the election, Lichtman was again featured in the *Times* and *Post* and *NPR*. The elite media also came back to him later in the year. He was interviewed, written about and spoken about in countless other venues – print, broadcast and online – including even *The Hollywood Reporter*. What better measure of heat?

The only interviewer I have found who focused sharply on the popular-electoral split was *NPR's* Robert Siegel, on the day after the election, which was the day when Hillary's lead in the popular vote surfaced.

He said, "Now, a question about that winning streak of yours. If I understand it, you claim predicting Al Gore's victory in 2000 as a win since he won the popular vote. But Hillary Clinton appears to also be winning the popular vote, and you don't claim a loss for predicting Donald Trump."

Before showing Lichtman's answer, let me explain that his 2016 prediction had been the most tepid he had ever made, that he did say before the election that Trump's peculiar, offensive characteristics might be the force that finally upsets the keys. He also said that he (Lichtman) might be wrong on how he called one key (more on that below) and that this was the first time he had ever hedged a prediction like that, which was true.

In his response to Siegel about not declaring a loss, he noted those statements and said: "So you had two forces colliding, which produced a win in the Electoral College, but essentially a tie, as far as I could tell, in the popular vote. We don't know how it's going to come out ultimately.

So, in fact, the keys came as close as you can to a contradictory election." That claim, of course, turned out to be weaker as Hillary's popular margin turned out to be almost three million votes (more than such presidents as John Kennedy, Richard Nixon in 1968 and Jimmy Carter).

Lichtman told me after the election that in his various interviews before and after the election he had not made a distinction between the popular and electoral votes.

But his first book makes the distinction twice in the first few pages. Page 8: "Because the Keys to the Presidency diagnose the national political environment, they correlate with the popular balloting, not with the votes of individual states in the Electoral College."

If in 2016 he was not talking about the popular vote, then he was not talking about his system. He was not talking about a system that had always been right before 2016. Yet the claim to have always been right was the best reason for giving him a prominent hearing now. If not about the popular vote, the system was not only wrong in 2000, but retroactively in 1876 and 1888.

If he is not talking about the popular vote, then he is not talking strictly about science anymore. He has made a leap beyond his system, beyond his data, a leap to celebrity predictor. Always before he – and I – insisted it was the system that was so compelling, because it was based on historical precedents, because it was open and anybody could apply it, and precisely because it got beyond individual views and instincts, beyond mere punditry.

Lichtman told me after the election that he now suspects that, while the keys did once predict the popular vote, they may now predict "something else." He said that will have to be tested with time. He speculated that as things stand now, the Democrats may win the popular vote in any close presidential election; so that's not what needs to be predicted. But if he's right about that, it's a post-2016 insight. He doesn't claim that it's a point he was trying to make in 2016-related interviews.

Why not simply admit that the failure he always knew had to come to any predictive system finally came in 2016 under incredible circumstances, when the keys were peculiarly close and hard to call?

So what happened in 2016?

Here, after all, we have a guy – Trump – of consistently record-breaking unpopularity. In the *CBS/New York Times* poll on "favorability" during the last two months of the campaign, Trump had, on average, 24 percent more people giving him an unfavorable rating than favorable. That put him in a class by himself among major-party presidential nominees in the 36-year history of the poll. Hillary's number was 16 percent, which tied her for second worst with incumbent George H. W. Bush in 1992, when he lost the election with 37.4 percent of the popular vote (in a three-way race).

After the election, Trump was judged by non-partisan fact-checking operations to be way, way in a class by himself for sheer dishonesty. See, for example, *FactCheck.org* on Dec. 21, 2015 where Trump was awarded the first-ever "King of the Whoppers" designation. Trump seemed an utterly appalling person to the big-name Republican columnists (George Will, Charles Krauthammer, David Brooks, Kathleen Parker, Ross Douthat). He seemed that way to Republican editorial boards across the country, almost none of which endorsed him even against the much hated Hillary Clinton. He seemed that way to dozens of high-profile Republican political figures – ranging from the party's establishment moderates to right-wing flame throwers – who called upon him to withdraw or who withheld their support.

And yet.

Although the keys were wrong, the fact that they stood so nearly alone in showing so much strength for Trump has generated interest in them and does make them worth pausing over.

The 2016 election ended Lichtman's three-election streak of making the prediction before the actual election year. Indeed, all the way through 2016 itself, he was struggling. Even floundering. Waiting. Hoping events and circumstances would clarify themselves. It was the toughest year for the keys, at least since 1992.

All year the Republicans had four of the six keys they needed: A big mid-term election for them had assured they had more seats in the House than before 2012. The Democrats could not run Obama again. Obama had not achieved a major change in national policy in his second term. And Hillary Clinton was not charismatic.

Meanwhile, there had been no major success in the realm of foreign policy. So a fifth key was poised to fall. Lichtman held out the possibility that a major success might develop. ISIS – the latest terrorist organization to emerge on a very major scale internationally – was presumed to be behind (in one way or another) a spate of attacks in Europe and the U.S. But it was on the defensive as to territory held. Lichtman felt if it were driven completely out of Iraq, that could be big. So that key couldn't be called early.

Actually, the overall international situation was decidedly bad. Might the other foreign policy key – the one about a failure by the administration – be turned against the Democrats, too? Syria was in unspeakable agony; Europe was deluged with desperate refugees; Iraq and Afghanistan were eluding Obamian solutions, and there were those periodic terrorist acts in the U.S. But the historical criterion for turning the key is a major setback to American interests. The Republicans pointed to a general decline in American influence, but it was hard to see American interests directly at stake in Syria, Iraq or Afghanistan in the absence of sizeable numbers of American troops there. And the domestic terrorism situation wasn't any worse than people seemed to expect in the modern era. So Lichtman was not calling that key against the Democrats.

Another key they might reasonably worry about was social unrest. Several cities had seen recent disturbances over police relations with black communities. Also, Trump's own rallies had an aura of near violence. In the end, however, there clearly wasn't enough to turn the key.

Hillary got both the economy keys. The election-year economy hummed along. And the overall growth rate in Obama's second term was better than that of the previous eight years, which had seen the great recession. Trump and other Republicans were campaigning as if the economy issue was entirely on their side – with Trump especially describing the exodus of jobs to other countries as if huge numbers of Americans were out of work. But jobs had grown in numbers very consistently under Obama. Probably the worst news about the economy was in the realm of stagnating salaries, especially where factory jobs had been replaced by lower-paying ones. But neither the Lichtman keys nor the Trump rhetoric went there.

What about the scandal key? It asks whether the "incumbent administration is untainted by major scandal." The Obama White House was thus untainted; the charge that the Internal Revenue Service was biased against conservatives didn't reach into the White House, a crucial standard.

There was an alleged scandal involving the nominee. The Republicans for years had insisted that Hillary's use of a private e-mail server as secretary of state was a major scandal, because she broke the rules, might have compromised national security and – a point emphasized by Trump – allegedly destroyed 30,000 e-mails the authorities were seeking. Her public exoneration (twice) by FBI Director James Comey of prosecutable offenses would seem to resolve the question of "major." There was no indictment. Moreover, to be considered major a scandal must appall beyond party lines. But Hillary's main opponent in the Democratic primaries, Sen. Bernie Sanders, had specifically said he didn't care about the "damn e-mails," a widely shared position.

We have considered 10 keys. The Republicans needed only one of the remaining three, if you give them the pending one about the absence of a major foreign policy success.

Before considering those three, perhaps this point is worth underlining: On foreign policy failure, social unrest, the economy and scandal, you can see problems for the Democrats, even if not big enough problems to turn the keys against them. On scandal, for example, the Republicans might not have crossed the key-turning threshold, but they did engage the media in the issue for years, and they did fuel their own people with outrage and did manage to achieve a situation in which Hillary's campaign was being regularly referred to as scandal-marred.

Where a key can't be turned against the incumbents, but you nevertheless sense that there's a problem for them, it's a good idea to wonder if the problem might show up indirectly in other keys. Might Hillary's "scandal" problem or the economy's very real flaws, for example, manifest themselves in, say, divisions within the governing party or the development of a strong third-party candidacy? Might even the sense that the international situation is bad – if not key-turning bad – matter because one of the candidates had been secretary of state?

The three keys we have not yet considered were incumbent party unity, the third-party key and the charisma key about the Republican candidate:

Party unity: As you may recall, almost always, when the party that holds the presidency has an uncontested or lightly contested nomination, that party wins; if it has a tough fight, it loses.

How to call the Clinton-Sanders fight? The key asks whether there's a "serious" contest for the nomination. Well, the outcome was never really in doubt. But "serious" is defined as a losing candidate getting more than a third of the votes on the first ballot at the national convention. Sanders did exceed that level, but he withdrew before the vote was official, and he called for Clinton's nomination by acclamation.

The convention really wasn't terribly divided, certainly not like the Democrats in 1968 or 1980, or the Republicans in 1976, the recent occasions upon which the key had been turned against the incumbents. But should convention unity be the main consideration, or should Sanders' surprising successes in the primaries be taken as a warning about the weakness of Hillary's appeal in the general election?

Lichtman ultimately decided it could be argued either way. He didn't make a call at all. It was the first time that happened with any key. (No rule says all the keys have to be called.)

By the time Lichtman made that decision, he was decidedly open to the possibility that this just wasn't the keys' year.

Third party: Again, with the third-party key, the standard is "significant." The only parties in play besides the big two were perennials: the Libertarians and the Greens, not typically considered "significant." But "significant" is defined as poised to get at least 5 percent of the vote. It was an unusual year. The Libertarian often topped that level in polls, because both major candidates were unpopular by any historical standard. But third parties tend to fade in the end. Tough call.

Republican charisma: I proposed to Lichtman that maybe Trump should be considered charismatic. On the premise that others might have had the same thought, here's my thinking:

It seemed clear that Trump had drawn support, especially early on, for reasons that had nothing to do with policy but were more about him as a person. After Trump's election and inauguration, the words populism and nationalism came to be habitually used about his views. Early in the campaign, though, they weren't. Journalists looking for a theme to his comments often couldn't find one and would characterize his speeches as simply incoherent. The buzz word associated with him was "outsider," as in "the year of the outsider in politics." But other outsiders – Dr. Ben Carson, Carly Fiorina – had a day and faded away. Trump was apparently just some people's idea of what a president should be like. And this fostered a special degree of excitement, at least in certain quarters.

Like so many in journalism and politics, I was deeply confused when Trump's campaign didn't collapse after he questioned John McCain's heroism; or viciously imitated a handicapped reporter; or insulted an opponent's looks and another opponent's wife's looks; or linked an opponent's father to John Kennedy's assassination. It also didn't collapse when Trump made incoherent "speeches;" or was revealed in a debate not to know what the nuclear triad is; or said he gets his information about foreign policy issues from "the shows" on television. It didn't collapse when Trump, upon being asked when asked whom he consulted about foreign policy, said "I'm speaking with myself, number one, because I have a very good brain;" or when he railed relentlessly against the outsourcing of jobs and then turned out to be a habitual practitioner of it. Likewise, the campaign didn't collapse when the media revealed him to be an incredibly ungenerous billionaire, even though he kept talking about big donations he planned to make; or when he called opponent Ben Carson "pathological" and likened him to a child molester in an undignified speech that involved Trump's belt; or when he asked, in that same speech, "How stupid are the people of Iowa?" because they seemed to be leaning to Carson. This list could go on. And on. Let's just say I didn't get it. Wasn't all this profoundly, obviously and disqualifyingly unpresidential from any ideological perspective?

Maybe I still don't get it, but my current guess is that I missed the beginning of the presidential campaign. I had not recognized as political events Trump's relentless and successful quest for attention over the years or, more specifically, the importance of his television program, wherein he played a big-boss figure. The candidates who collapse after a couple of public embarrassments are the ones the public is just getting to know; they make a bad early impression. But Trump's 2015 impression on the public was way beyond early. That, I guess, is what I didn't get. Or part of it.

Then he apparently won some new supporters in the campaign because of his persona. When, in the Republican debates, some of us saw a policy ignoramus, an egomaniac, a petty insulter, a demagogue, an authoritarian extremist and divider, others saw a leader. He stood out – in a way that was apparently not all bad – from a Republican field lacking in president-seeming figures with presidential resumes. In discussing the difficulties of the campaign later, former Florida Gov. Jeb Bush spoke of having to compete with this "larger than life" figure. Well, "larger than life" is a concept that has at least a little in common with "charismatic."

Fairly early in 2015, a friend told me about a conversation he had had with a woman in Oklahoma, a woman of no apparent expertise or specialization in politics. In the conversation, my friend had laughed at the idea of a Trump presidency, and this woman said, "Oh, no. He's going to be president. I'm never wrong about things like this." I, of course, thought that ranked with the dumbest things I had ever heard, and my response was that of a Lichtmaniac: All these people who tell you they are wonderful predictors always forget their failures and always fail to record their predictions in writing, so that you have to just take their word for it. But as the political season progressed and my expectations were blown out of the water, and Trump prospered, I thought more and more about that woman. She apparently had a sort of big-picture sense of things – insight without mountains of data, perhaps best characterized as common sense.

For well into the Republican primaries, the words populism and nationalism were not particularly associated with Trump. The buzz word was "outsider." And the most frequent characterization of his speeches was incoherent.

It is a pretty good – though not perfect – generalization that in presidential primaries voters tend to go with the person who is already most like a president – a former vice president, say, or Senate leader, or somebody who has been on the national stage via previous presidential bids. Trump had spent a lot of time on the national stage, that is, had become a national figure, certainly more so than his Republican competitors. And a lot of people apparently saw his accomplishments in life as more impressive – and more indicative of leadership skills – than those of the others. And beyond that, he was simply dominating the scene, getting all the attention, shaping the course of debate. He seemed most like a president. I guess.

Nevertheless, Lichtman – and friends to whom I proposed that Trump was charismatic – saw more meaning in the fact that Trump's personality had an off-putting effect on huge numbers of people. Millions simply loathed him. They wouldn't have been caught dead watching his television show. The previous modern charismatics – FDR, JFK, Obama – stirred no such hatred except among people who hated their politics. Turning the key for Trump wouldn't have been consistent with its historical usage.

Still, as with other keys that couldn't quite be turned against Hillary, there seemed to be a problem for her. It lay somewhere near a point Trump had articulated in January, 2016: that he could stand in the middle of Fifth Avenue and shoot somebody and not lose any support. Though he was widely trashed for making the observation, many had made it before him. And nobody would have said it about Hillary.

At any rate, such were the keys. You can see that calling them was tough. Close.

Lichtman didn't make his call until almost three weeks after Labor Day, which holiday had been the time of his latest call until then, in 1992. Finally, he concluded that there was no major Obama success to be had in foreign policy, which gave the Republicans that key. Five. And he made his move on the third-party key. He wrongly guessed the Libertarian would get 5 percent. The correct answer was 3.

So Trump got his six keys, the bare minimum number, with the bare minimum confidence.

We come to irony (admittedly never far away in politics): If Lichtman had turned the third party key correctly, he'd still be able to claim his system has never been wrong, which would be a remarkable claim. But he'd be making it a vacuum. He would have called a Hillary victory when everybody was doing that. And he would have been right in a technical sense of little interest. If the popular and electoral votes are going to diverge so widely, then calling the popular winner is like accurately predicting the attendance figures at a ball game: not really what people are looking for.

If, in September, you were sitting in Lichtman's place – with no great confidence that you knew who was going to win what – you would most certainly have known that calling Trump (to win anything) would be in your interest. It would create a splash during the campaign. And if he won in either form of voting, you'd be a star. If he won nothing, it would just be the setback that was inevitable and had been delayed a remarkably long time and finally came at a time when everybody else was wrong, too.

Nevertheless, Lichtman did not make the Trump prediction for for self-serving purposes. If he had been looking for a way to call Trump, he could easily have justified labeling the Democrats divided, giving Trump the second key. I had all year felt the keys were leaning toward Trump.

At any rate, the credit Lichtman got was sometimes amazing. In the Post's Cillizza column mentioned at the start of this chapter, that writer offered some background info: "Lichtman is a distinguished professor of history at American University who, most notably, has developed a full-proof and time-tested system to predict the winner of presidential elections. In this election, his system suggested, narrowly, that Donald Trump would win – at a time when you couldn't find ANYONE willing to say that on the record."

"Full-proof" is apparently a typo or misspelling of "fool-proof." "Fool-proof" is a foolish appraisal. Certainly Lichtman had never claimed that. But the term shows you something about the forces at work as this is written.

What to do with the fact that the keys made their biggest splash ever – by miles – by being wrong for the first time?

Let's call it rough justice. If the only time the keys are clearly wrong in 32 years is when there's a split between the popular and electoral votes, that's an extraordinary record. As far as I have been able to determine, it is an unmatched record. Indeed, it is a not-remotely-close-to-matched record. Meanwhile, the keys give us a whole new – and infinitely better – way of understanding what matters in American politics. They deserve the attention they are finally getting, even if the timing is decidedly peculiar.

———

What follows is the argument that, notwithstanding their failure to predict in 2016, the keys offer essential and too rare insight into events that perplexed so many for so long and that will be debated for longer.

If the keys did not prevail, their logic did. And their logic is what's most important.

Here's one widely held theory about 2016: that the explanation for Trump's surprising strength in both the primaries and the general election lay in the specific economic conditions of the times, especially the conditions of the white working class. David Brooks, the "Never Trump," moderate Republican columnist for the *New York Times*, used the word "declinism" and declared after Trump's nomination that he was going to take to the road to seek a better understanding of the effects of that phenomenon on American life. After the election, the fact that Trump did better among white working-class voters in the Midwest and Pennsylvania than, say, Mitt Romney in 2012 was perhaps the most widely cited reason for his victory. And there was much talk about a populist, nationalist, protectionist, anti-elitist, anti-establishment movement inspired by Trump's rhetoric.

And yet, upon analysis, the first fact that stands out about Trump's victory is simply that Republicans voted Republican. That's where the huge bulk of his popular and electoral votes came from. He won all the red states, and most of them comfortably. In a normal year, that might be taken for granted. But the huge gap between Republican voters and Republican "leaders" must be noted. Look at Ohio (not necessarily a red state, but close enough for the point). The popular Republican senator seeking re-election (and winning big), Rob Portman, said he wouldn't vote for Trump. The popular Republican governor, John Kasich (who had trounced Trump in the primary), and the state party chairman, and the Republican newspapers were all hostile. Didn't matter. At all. Stunningly big Trump victory.

Maybe the explanation for partisan voting was concern about the Supreme Court; maybe it was hatred of Hillary or just garden-variety partisanship. But the notion that it represented an embrace of a new set of Trumpian, anti-establishment values is hard to credit. If we're talking about voters who always vote Republican, why look for some new force at work? Those voters didn't change their behavior. Does anybody believe they would not have voted for, say, Jeb Bush if he had been the nominee?

In the various primaries, Trump seldom won a majority until the end of the season, when other candidacies had died officially or were near death. But, OK, let's say there was some philosophical appeal there, given that he did win many primaries. To use that appeal as an explanation for Republican votes by Republican voters in the general election makes no sense.

The fact that Republican voters have recently proved willing to vote for both Mitt Romney and Donald Trump in November demonstrates the importance of party labels *as opposed to* political postures or policy positions (or personalities).

Of course, Trump needed some non-Republican votes to win even the Electoral College. How did such an unpopular person get them? Here, after all, we're talking about voters who were *not* obsessed with the Supreme Court and did not have a long seething hatred for Hillary, and were telling the pollsters all along that they didn't like Trump.

Trump's substantial Electoral College margin was provided by three states in the old "Rust Belt": Michigan, Pennsylvania and Wisconsin, all of which were decided by less than one percent of the vote. They had been won by Democrats in recent presidential elections (including 2012, when times were tougher), and the pollsters generally had them favoring Hillary pretty much all along.

They were so close that Hillary's defeat in them can be attributed to all manner of factors. For example, she ran worse than Obama did in 2012 among young people and blacks. But if you're looking at the region as a whole – not just the paper-thin states – you can't help but be struck by her problem with white blue-collar workers.

Ohio is most instructive. Nobody could have predicted that, in a year when the Democrats were winning the popular vote by a couple of percentage points, they would lose Ohio by 8, especially given the hostility of the Republican establishment to Trump. That was the biggest margin in Ohio in a presidential election since 1988, which wasn't even a close election nationally. The 2016 margin seems to take Ohio out of the "swing state" category that it had characterized so notoriously for so long. Maybe it doesn't. Some people think the Democrats just have to be sure to nominate free-trade bashers like their twice elected Senator Sherrod Brown. What's clear is that Hillary's trouncing in Ohio was too big to be attributed to anything other than her problems with the white working class, and that the same political problem was at work elsewhere in the region.

And yet, if Trump's unusual pitch did him some good with white working-class swing voters in certain states (keeping in mind that we don't know how a more traditional Republican would have done), it may also have caused him some problems elsewhere. When you look at the surprising gap between Ohio and the nation as a whole, you have to wonder whether, by fashioning a pitch so powerful in one region, Trump lost votes in others. When he demonized Mexico and illegal immigrants, did he lose in the popular vote even as he gained in the Electoral College?

Most specifically, Trump did badly on the coasts, where, it has long been noted, people tend to have a different orientation toward the outside world for various reasons, including that they are closer to it. And the decline of American manufacturing hasn't been as big a phenomenon there. And there are simply fewer white voters without a college education. To many voters there – this theory would hold – Trump's antagonism toward the outside world didn't resonate, or even backfired.

Of course, the places where Trump lost are just naturally more Democratic. But that doesn't appear to be the whole story.

In the week before the election, the polls generally showed Trump losing the three crucial states he ended up winning so narrowly. Apparently the late deciders tended to go for Trump. Specifically, as Nate Silver of the FiveThirtyEight website reported in his election post-mortem, those who decided in the last week went for Trump by 29 percentage points in Wisconsin, 17 in Pennsylvania and 11 in Michigan.

On the other hand, Silver lists 11 states, besides the District of Columbia, where Hillary met or exceeded poll-generated expectations: California, New York, Illinois, New Jersey, Massachusetts, Hawaii, Nevada, New Mexico, Oregon, Rhode Island and Washington. We're talking seriously Democratic territory.

So the late deciders – presumably non-partisan voters – went one way is some places and the other way in others. Why? An answer derived from the logic of the keys would hold that the case for change – the final subject at work on some voters – resonated better in some places than others.

Specifically, it looks as though the trade-off Trump made – knowingly or otherwise – between the Midwest and the coasts worked. If the idea was to give up votes in the states that were hopeless for him anyway, while picking up votes in states where every vote mattered, it was brilliant.

So perhaps what's most special about 2016 is that it provided an unprecedented opportunity for a candidate to play the Electoral College (or to unknowingly benefit from its nature).

Of course, this book promotes the view that campaign strategies don't affect the outcomes of elections. The theory is that the circumstances of any given year mitigate very strongly in favor of one party being able to put together a winning coalition. It is that both sides will get the most out of their political circumstances, and no more. Strategic efforts to undermine the overarching forces at work are likely – in the rare cases where they have any impact – to do as much harm as good, to result in trade-offs that don't affect the overall outcome. In this case, though, the trade-off did work, because the Electoral College makes some votes much more important than others.

Very seldom will campaign rhetoric move a decisive number of voters in November. But the circumstances were just right.

At any rate, Trump won through the usual combination of partisan votes and change votes. Why those forces count for more than his unpopular personal characteristics is a subject for a more ambitious book than this one. But given those characteristics, we now know more clearly than ever just how monumentally powerful the partisanship and change factors are.

———

Let's check back in with Nate Silver – the highest profile predictor in the country (see the previous chapter) – and his FiveThirtyEight website. In the wake of the election, Silver wrote a piece labeled "Why FiveThirtyEight Gave Trump a Better Chance than Almost Anyone."

He wrote: "Our final forecast, issued early Tuesday evening, had Trump with a 29 percent chance of winning the Electoral College. By comparison, other models tracked by *The New York Times* put Trump's odds at 15 percent, 8 percent, 2 percent and less than 1 percent. And betting markets put Trump's chances at just 18 percent at midnight on Tuesday, when Dixville Notch, New Hampshire, cast its votes."

For the record, however, Hillary had been doing better with Silver earlier. On Oct. 12 Silver had said, "We're spending a lot of time these days diagnosing whether Donald Trump's position in the polls is merely bad or still getting worse. Most of the evidence on Wednesday — which included the first dusting of state polls since the second presidential debate, on Sunday night — fell into the 'still getting worse' bucket. Trump's chances are down to 14 percent in our polls-only forecast (against an 86 percent chance for Hillary Clinton) and to 17 percent, a record low for Trump, in our polls-plus forecast."

In short, Silver simply blew it, too. True, he was indeed attacked in, for example, the liberal *Huffington Post* in the days before the election for being way too timid in calling a Hillary victory. *HuffPo* said Florida would come in for Hillary at dinner time on Election Night. It went for Trump. But *HuffPo* isn't the standard. Right or wrong is the standard.

Silver defends his methods (reliance on poll averages studied for their meaning over years) and insists the national polls weren't that wrong. He also notes, as reported above, what happened with undecided voters in the final days. He does have some good points.

When he says the national polls weren't far off, he means the last polls. Mid-October polls showed Hillary's lead nearing double digits. There were certainly earlier periods when things were closer, like 2 points. (Specifically, the *CNN* poll went from a 2-point lead to a 9-point lead after the Trump sex scandals.) What is hardest to explain is that media confidence about the outcome didn't fade when the polls narrowed from time to time. After all, not long before, in Britain, the polls showed the referendum to withdraw from the European Union (Brexit) to be losing by a non-squeaker, but it won a non-squeaker. Sometimes close polls are right, and sometimes they're wrong. The fact that most pollsters go in the same direction on a given race means something but not all that much. (That point is granted by Silver, who says the pollsters often copy each other's mistakes).

Blame the nearly universal failure of the political community to foresee any sort of Trump victory partly on Silver, who is enormously influential. But a bigger problem was a chronic, incurable condition: the determination of the designated political "experts" to believe they know far more than they really know.

It isn't as though they didn't have evidence for their predictions. They kept pointing to the campaigns and to campaign events as their evidence.

Here's another quote from James Carville, the high-profile Democratic campaign veteran who has a way with words.

"'The Trump campaign is not a bad campaign. It's not a messed-up

campaign. It's not a dysfunctional campaign. There is no campaign. Everybody that's done this for a living and got paid to do it is, like, 'Oh, my gosh, suppose this works. We're all rendered useless.' He will have destroyed an entire profession."

That quote was reported by Lizzie Widdicombe in the *New Yorker* of Aug. 22, 2016, but Carville was making the point elsewhere, too. He was not doing a favor for a non-entity writing a book called "Campaigns Don't Count." I swear I have never met the man. But he does make my point more effectively than any similar number of words in this book, I suppose.

In truth, however, the people who make their livings off political campaigns will not fade away as a result of Trump's victory. But maybe a few young people and a few candidates will hear the Carville quote from time to time and be affected. Let it live.

The 2016 campaign utterly befuddled the political professionals in journalism as much as those in campaign work. In *The New York Times*, the *Washington Post* and *Politico*, an online publication for political obsessives, everything Donald Trump did was taken as yet more evidence that he was an incredibly inept candidate who was blowing it: He trashed the parents of a Muslim soldier who died in service of this country. He raised the subject of Bill Clinton's sex life only to be charged with sexual abuse by almost a dozen women himself. He debated. He got in political bed with Russian leader Vladimir Putin. He failed to offer a remotely convincing reason for not revealing his tax returns or for long questioning Barack Obama's citizenship. He campaigned in states where he didn't seem to have a chance. He changed and re-changed his campaign staff. He failed to be sufficiently serious about raising and spending money. He seemed not to recognize that he wasn't just talking to Republican primary voters anymore. The list of his alleged campaign screw-ups was endless.

After the election, the inevitable debate about what caused its outcome focused, inevitably, on campaign-season events that were problems for the loser. As this book has attempted to document, that's always the way it is — the setbacks for the winner never happened.

OK, it's reasonable enough to suspect that Hillary Clinton was hurt by FBI Director James Comey's October decision to announce the re-opening of an investigation into her use of a private e-mail system as secretary of state. The renewal certainly made Trump and the Republicans unabashedly jubilant.

When Comey announced a week before the election that Hillary had been cleared again, the media and the politicians tended to think the issue hadn't done Hillary much harm. Nate Silver reported on the Sunday before the election that Hillary's decline after the re-opening "has leveled off, and her lead has held steady over the past several days." After the election, though, she and others said the whole Comey thing had stopped her momentum, changed the subject to bad headlines and might even have affected the decisions of early voters.

On top of that issue – in the anti-Hillary category – there were news stories that resulted from the disclosure of various Democratic e-mails that had been hacked by Russians. These stories reported things like spats among various Democrats, infighting at the Clintons' charitable foundation and criticisms of Hillary by Democrats. One Democrat was quoted as calling Hillary's political instincts "suboptimal." The Democratic campaign was revealed to know in advance about one question to be asked by a voter at a debate. Earlier in the year, embarrassing hacked revelations about Democratic infighting had caused the departure of the party's national chair.

In the campaign, the hacked stories seldom showed up as lead stories of the day. They were not widely seen at the time as devastating to Hillary. (If they had been, after all, people would not have been shocked by the outcome of the election.) Personally, I found them boring: too far inside baseball even for me. But, again, afterward some people said the steady stream of stories sapped Democratic energy and momentum. It's a lame argument.

One simply cannot make the case that the hacks had remotely the impact on the public as the really big splash of the campaign: the Oct. 8 revelation of an audiotape in which a 59-year-old Donald Trump bragged of grabbing women by the "pussy" or kissing them or "anything," and being able to get away with it because he was a "star." In response to this revelation, Trump declared that this was just "locker room talk," and that he didn't really treat women like that. But then about 10 women came forth with the allegation that he had treated them like that.

It cannot be exaggerated how big – how unprecedentedly big – this was at the time. Several dozen big-name Republicans called upon Trump to withdraw from the race. The list included former Secretary of State Condoleezza Rice and U.S. senators from Utah, Idaho, Nebraska, Alaska, South Dakota and Colorado. Typical was Colorado Sen. Cory Gardner, who said, "If Donald Trump wishes to defeat Hillary Clinton, he should do the only thing that will allow us to do so – step aside." That was the conventional wisdom of the moment about how the race was going.

Meanwhile other Republican senators or Senate candidates – from New Hampshire, Ohio and Arizona – withdrew their support from Trump, without asking him to leave the race. The Arizonan was John McCain, the party's nominee for president in 2008 and still one of its biggest figures. House Speaker Paul Ryan announced he would be unwilling to appear with Trump.

Any devotee of the Lichtman keys believes that news stories that break out during campaigns don't matter in the end. Each candidate experiences his or her embarrassments, but, after a long, long campaign, that all becomes a blur to voters. It all washes out. Voters conclude that both candidates are flawed, and both are pretty impressive, and other factors rule.

But the "locker room" tape seemed at the time to be the exception. I found that I couldn't tell friends to expect it to wash out. That was all but unimaginable. The prediction would have seemed other-worldly, even to me. This one was just too big.

But it washed out. By the end, it was simply gone. The widely expected collapse of support for Trump among Republican women, especially, didn't materialize. The views of Trump's Republican critics ultimately held no water with Republican voters. Most symbolic of the issue's passing: Some of the very politicians who had called upon Trump to withdraw were now publicly back on board, however awkward that was. Sen. Deb Fischer of Nebraska said, "I put out a statement... with regard to Mr. Trump's comments. I felt they were disgusting. I felt they were unacceptable, and I never said I was not voting for our Republican ticket."

So are we supposed to believe that the bad news for Trump washed out, but the bad news for Hillary didn't, despite being so much milder, and, in large measure, temporary? That requires, I suppose, holding that Hillary's ultimate problem was that her bad news came last. But, of course, if she had won the election, the conventional analysts would have pointed out that the good news for her – Comey's final conclusion – happened last.

The truth is that the effort to blame Hillary's campaign-season problems for her loss, despite the constant stream of horrible news for Trump, is just way too opportunistic. It grows out of the holy discredited assumption that if somebody lost a close election, it must be because of campaign events.

Even aside from Trump's alleged blunders and embarrassments, Hillary's campaign was universally judged during the campaign to be better. By all accounts, she had the better convention, being vouched for in a series of compelling speeches by stars like Michelle Obama and Bill Clinton, some of whom also eviscerated Trump compellingly. Hillary came out of the conventions with a polling lead in the high single digits. Then she won all the debates in the eyes of the public, judging by the polls. She had a decidedly more united party. She spent more money, had more big-name support, not only in politics but in show business. She had a far, far better "ground game," that is, more people deployed to work for her on Election Day, a factor that all manner political analysts said would resolve the election if it turned out to be the least bit close. These are the kinds of factors that the professionals talk about when they talk about and judge a campaign.

It won't do to point out in response that, after all, Hillary Clinton won the popular vote by millions. She lost the crucial swing states where the election – the campaign – was fought. True, some of those states were painfully close. But that's precisely when and where campaigns and ground game and all that are supposed to matter most.

Like all campaigners, Hillary committed her share of screw-ups. She stupidly trashed half of Trump's supporters as a "basket of deplorables." She had fewer and smaller campaign rallies. But note the fundamental characteristic of that list: It is *not* endless; it is short. Unmistakably, if you described both campaigns to a panel of political professionals and asked them to guess who won, she'd win. No contest.

———————

The 2016 election highlighted the limitations of a remarkably successful and extraordinarily revealing predictive scheme, but it also highlighted some essential truths behind it. And, whatever else one might say about it, it did get that essence-revealing quote out of Carville.

Following the course of the keys over four decades has, admittedly, been a learning experience for an advocate of them. I've tried to capture the experience in this book. After all, the whole thing started with a system predicting the outcomes of U.S. Senate elections. That system – stunningly effective in its time – turned out to be time-bound. An era arrived in which some election years favored a particular party more strongly than could be captured by existing keys. The Senate keys had been developed by looking at history only back to 1970 (from 1982), not back to the dawning of the current two party system. Perhaps predictably enough, the resulting keys turned out only to work for a while.

As for the presidential keys, they do turn out to be a little harder to turn – more subjective – than Lichtman originally argued, and I originally believed. Moreover, the very close calls – the "one-key" elections" that Lichtman was trying to avoid when he developed 13 keys – turned out to happen occasionally anyway. And, yes, the keys met their match in 2016, with 1992 also being a debatable call.

Does the 2016 failure of the keys – and the general difficulty in turning them in that year – suggest that something has changed about the times, something that obviates the keys (something other than popular vote/Electoral College issues mentioned above)?

Certainly the explosion of social media must be confronted. It has been widely cited as an explanation or partial explanation for the Trump phenomenon. Trump was able to bypass the mainstream media as nobody before with his tweeting, mainly. Meanwhile, factual nonsense distributed on social media by his campaign and others was unusually rampant. The keys, after all, are based on the importance of facts. Are facts becoming less important? Surely, Trump's flamboyant contempt for truth will become a model for somebody else.

That suggests another possible game-changer: Perhaps Trump's brand of demagogy, virulent dishonesty, tribalism, populism and charisma (or whatever you call it) would have flourished in any other year, too. We just hadn't seen it before. Now we have.

But my further speculations would be of no more value than anybody else's. Because I've been impressed again and again with the durability of the keys system, put me down as skeptical that much is going to change. But that's all I've got.

What can be said now is that the 2016 election highlighted the limits of the keys, but that the case for them was never that they resolve all questions. It was – and is – that they provide a framework for understanding American politics that is hugely more true than the one used universally by journalists and political practitioners alike. The keys provide an opportunity to tell the American people what is really going on in our presidential elections – an opportunity just about everybody resolutely rejects.

Index

174, 182, 183, 184, 190, 191, 192, 194

DeCell, Ken 40, 69, 166

defense buildup 52

deficit xvi, 10, 13, 39, 61, 67, 101, 102, 134

Democratic xvi, 9, 11, 12, 13, 14, 17, 18, 21, 22, 32, 33, 34, 40, 41, 42, 43, 45, 46, 54, 60, 61, 62, 64, 65, 66, 67, 76, 79, 83, 84, 87, 89, 91, 92, 93, 94, 95, 99, 103, 104, 106, 110, 113, 118, 124, 125, 127, 129, 131, 132, 133, 136, 139, 140, 150, 159, 160, 161, 162, 163, 167, 168, 175, 180, 188, 190, 192

Democratic convention 9, 13, 14, 46, 60, 95, 99, 103

Democrat(s) 9, 12, 13, 15, 17, 21, 24, 25, 29, 32, 33, 34, 35, 39, 40, 45, 48, 51, 54, 55, 58, 60, 62, 63, 67, 75, 76, 77, 79, 80, 81, 83, 84, 89, 93, 95, 99, 105, 106, 107, 109, 112, 116, 118, 119, 123, 124, 125, 126, 130, 131, 132, 133, 134, 135, 136, 137, 138, 139, 140, 145, 147, 150, 156, 158, 160, 161, 165, 166, 168, 169, 176, 177, 178, 179, 180, 181, 185, 187, 192

Detroit News 111

DeWine, Mike 128, 129, 150

Diemer, Tom 110

District of Columbia 188

Dixville Notch, New Hampshire 189

Dole, Bob 42, 48, 49, 76, 77, 121, 123, 130

"don't know" 2, 7, 12, 146, 173, 176, 188

Douthat, Ross 178

Dow Jones average 25

drugs 10, 102

Dukakis, Michael 40, 42, 58, 61, 66, 150

Dukes of Hazzard, The 129

Dwight Eisenhower 45, 56, 57, 79, 107, 113, 120, 161

earthquakes 24

Economist, The 85

economy 3, 10, 13, 19, 20, 21, 25, 36, 37, 40, 42, 49, 50, 51, 52, 60, 61, 67, 69, 72, 73, 75, 76, 84, 96, 99, 100, 101, 102, 104, 106, 107, 109, 110, 111, 112, 113, 121, 122, 132, 139, 140, 142, 143, 156, 162, 165, 168, 172, 179, 180

editorial page xiv

Edsall, Thomas B. 59

Edwards, George 56

Edwards, John 161

Einstein, Albert 153

Eisenhower, Karl 21

Electoral College vii, 44, 69, 97, 98, 99, 101, 102, 117, 176, 177, 187, 188, 189, 195

Elias, Thomas D. 86

e-mail 180, 191, 192

endorsements 15, 144

environmentalists 40

Estrich, Susan 80

European Union 190

Evening Standard (London) 84, 85, 151

exit polls 106, 120

experts xiii, xiv, 1, 2, 3, 11, 23, 26, 36, 59, 63, 65, 105, 115, 123, 190

"Extremism in defense of liberty is no vice" 133

FactCheck.org 178

Fair, Ray 19

faith-based 82, 108, 112

Printed in the United States
By Bookmasters